HOW TO
STUDY
THE BIBLE

HOW TO
STUDY
THE BIBLE

John MacArthur

MOODY PUBLISHERS

CHICAGO

Interior Design: Ragont Design
Cover Design: John Hamilton Design
Cover Image: Spohn Matthieu/Getty

ISBN: 978-0-8024-5303-7

We hope you enjoy this book from Moody Publishers. Our goal is to provide high-quality, thought-provoking books and products that connect truth to your real needs and challenges. For more information on other books and products written and produced from a biblical perspective, go to www.moodypublishers.com or write to:

Moody Publishers
820 N. LaSalle Boulevard
Chicago, IL 60610

3 5 7 9 10 8 6 4 2

Printed in the United States of America

CONTENTS

1

THE POWER
of the WORD in the
BELIEVER'S LIFE
Part 1

It is vital for every Christian to know how to study the Bible. You should be able to dig into God's Word yourself to glean and gain all the riches the Bible contains. I often think of the words of Jeremiah who said, "Your words were found, and I ate them, and Your Word was to me the joy and rejoicing of my heart" (Jer. 15:16a). The Word of God is a tremendous resource. Christians should not be handicapped in their ability to study God's Word for themselves. So we are going to be examining how to study the Bible. But first, we should see why it is important to study it.

Walter Scott, a British novelist and poet and a great

Christian, was dying when he said to his secretary, "Bring me the Book." His secretary looked at the thousands of books in his library and said, "Dr. Scott, which book?" He said, "The Book, the Bible—the only Book for a dying man." And I would have to add that the Bible is not just the only Book for a *dying* man, but it's the only Book for a *living* man, because it is the Word of life, as well as the hope in death.

So we come to the Word of God with a tremendous sense of excitement and anticipation. But before I share with you how to study the Bible, I must tell you about the authority of the Word of God. Then you will see the importance of Bible study. Also, we must state from the very beginning that the Scripture is the Word of God. It is not man's opinion, it is not human philosophy, it is not somebody's ideas, it is not a pooling of the best thoughts of the best men—it is the Word of God. Consequently, there are several things we need to realize about it.

The Attributes of the Bible

1. The Bible Is Infallible

The Bible, in its entirety, has no mistakes. Specifically, in its original autographs it is without errors. In Psalm 19:7 the Bible says of itself, "The law of the Lord is perfect." It is flawless because God wrote it—and He is flawless. Therefore, if God wrote the Bible, and if He is the ultimate authority, and if His character is flawless, then the Bible is flawless and is the ultimate authority. You see, because God is perfect, the original autographs, the original transmissions of the Word of God, must also be perfect. So, the Bible is infallible, and that's the first reason to study it; it is the only Book that never makes a mistake—everything it says is the truth.

Not only is it *infallible*, but there's a second word we use in describing the Bible, and that is:

2. The Bible Is Inerrant

The Bible is not only infallible in total, but inerrant in its parts. In Proverbs 30:5–6 it says, "Every word of God is pure.... Do not add to His words, lest He rebuke you, and you be found a liar." So every Word of God is pure and true.

The Bible is not only *infallible* and *inerrant*, but:

3. The Bible Is Complete

Nothing needs to be added to the Bible. Now that may be a surprise to some people, because there are those today who believe we need additional revelation. There exists a philosophy-theology known as neo-orthodoxy. It tells us that the Bible was simply a comment in its day on human spiritual experiences, and today humans are still having spiritual experiences. Therefore, humanity needs another comment. One writer said that we need a Bible to be written today, just as we did when the Bible we have in our hands was written, because we need somebody to comment on what God is doing now. He also said that when Tom or Mary stand up in your church and say, "Thus says the Lord," they are as equally inspired as Isaiah, Jeremiah, or any of the other prophets (J. Rodman Williams, *The Era of the Spirit*, Logos International, 1971).

In other words, they claim that the Bible is not complete. That's the current philosophical-theological thought. Let's look at the end of the last book of the Bible, the book of Revelation: "If anyone adds to these things, God will add to him the plagues that are written in this book; and if anyone takes away from the words of the book of this prophecy, God shall take away his part from the Book of Life, from the holy city, and from the things which are written in this book (22:18b–19). The Bible ends with a warning not to take away anything, and not to add anything. That's a testimony of its completeness. It is *infallible* in its total, *inerrant* in its parts, and it is *complete*.

A fourth way to describe the Bible's attributes is to say that:

4. The Bible Is Authoritative

If it is perfect and complete, then it is the last Word—the final authority. Isaiah 1:2 says, "Hear, O heavens, and give ear, O earth! For the Lord has spoken." When God speaks everybody listens and obeys, because His is the final authority. We can discuss its implications, its applications, and its meanings, but we shouldn't discuss whether or not it is true.

In John 8 Jesus was confronted by some of the Jewish leaders, and there were other people present. Verses 30b–31 say, "Many believed in him. Then Jesus said to those Jews who believed Him, 'If you abide in My word, you are My disciples indeed.'" In other words, He demanded response to His Word because it *is* authoritative.

In Galatians 3:10 it says, "Cursed is everyone who does not continue in all things which are written in the book of the law, to do them." That's a tremendous claim to absolute authority. In James 2:9–10 we read, "But if you show partiality, you commit sin, and are convicted by the law as transgressors. For whoever shall keep the whole law, and yet stumble in one point, he is guilty of all." To violate the Bible at one point is to break God's law. The Bible is authoritative in every part.

The Bible is *infallible, inerrant, complete, authoritative.* As a result, we can make an additional claim that:

5. *The Bible Is Sufficient*

The Bible is sufficient for a number of things. First it is sufficient for our salvation. In 2 Timothy 3:15 Paul said to Timothy, "And that from childhood you have known the Holy Scriptures, which are able to make you wise for salvation through faith which is in Christ Jesus." First of all, the Bible is *sufficient* to "make you wise for salvation." Ask yourself this question: What is more important than salvation? Nothing! It is the greatest reality in the universe—and the Bible reveals that salvation.

Second, 2 Timothy 3:16 (emphases added) indicates the Bible is sufficient for our perfection: "All scripture is given by inspiration of God, and is profitable *for doctrine*"—that means "teaching, principles of wisdom, divine standards, or divine truths"; "*for reproof*"—that means you're able to go to someone and say, "Hey, you're out of line. You can't behave like that; there's a standard and you're not keeping it." Scripture is also profitable "*for correction*"—that says to the person you've just reproved, "Now don't do that, do this instead; this is the right path." You teach, you reprove, you show the correct way—and further it is profitable "*for instruction in righteousness*." Now you point to the new way and show them how to walk in it. The Bible is a fantastic book. It can take somebody who doesn't know God, who isn't saved, and then save them. Then it will teach them, reprove them when they do wrong, point out the right thing to do, and then show them how to walk in that right path.

The result is stated in verse 17: "That the man of God may be complete, thoroughly equipped for every good work." The incredible reality of the Bible is that it is *sufficient* to do the whole job.

Third, the Bible is sufficient in its hope. In Romans 15:4 it says, "For whatever things were written before [referring to the Bible] were written for our learning, that we through patience and comfort of the Scriptures might have hope." The Bible is the source of patience and comfort, ultimately giving us hope now and forever.

Finally, the Bible is sufficient in its blessing. I think of the tremendous text of James 1:25, "But he who looks into the perfect law of liberty [the Scripture] and continues in it, and is not a forgetful hearer but a doer of the work, this one will be blessed in what he does." When you read it and then do it—you're blessed.

Back in James 1:21, James says that we should "receive with meekness the implanted word, which is able to save your souls." The Greek text literally means it is able to "save your life." In other words, it will save your life if you receive the Word of God. I think by that he means that it will give you the fullest life imaginable. But it is possible also for a Christian who doesn't obey the Word of God to lose his life. In 1 Corinthians 11 some of the Christians in Corinth violated the practice of the Lord's Table or Communion, and He took them home. Verse 30 says, "For this reason many are weak and sick among you, and many sleep [are dead]." Ananias and Sapphira disobeyed God's command and dropped dead in front of the whole church (Acts 5:1–11). So James said, "If you receive the implanted word, and you obey it, and you continue in it, it has an incredible way of perfecting you, of blessing you, of saving your life." All these things are true of the Word of God.

6. The Bible Is Effective

Consider the words of Isaiah 55:11: "So shall My word be that goes forth from My mouth; It shall not return unto Me void, but it shall accomplish what I please." God's Word is effective. One of the incredible things about being a teacher of the Word of God is that it will do what it promises to do.

I often wonder about the door-to-door salesperson who tries to demonstrate his product, and then it doesn't work right. I remember the story of the lady who lived in the country, and a vacuum cleaner salesman came by with a high-pressure sales pitch. He said, "I have the greatest product you've ever seen. This vacuum cleaner will eat up anything. In fact, if I don't control it, it will suck up your carpet." Before she could say anything, he said. "I want to give you a demonstration."

He immediately went to the fireplace and threw some of the ashes in the middle of the carpet. He also had a bag of stuff which he dumped on the carpet. Then he said, "I want you to watch it suck every bit of that up." She stood there aghast. Finally, he said to her, "If it doesn't suck up every bit of this, I'll eat it all with a spoon." She looked him right in the eyes and said, "Well sir, start eating, because we ain't got no electricity."

It's pretty tough to have your product be inoperable or ineffective. But that never happens with the Bible—it is *always* effective—it always does exactly what it says it will do. That's a tremendous reality about the Scripture.

First Thessalonians 1:5 is a great verse about the effectiveness of the Scripture: "For our gospel did not come to you in word only, but also in power, and in the Holy Spirit and in much assurance." In other words, when you hear the Word of God, it isn't just words. When the Word goes forth it has power; it is powered by the Holy Spirit, and we have the assurance that it will do what it says.

So far we have seen that the Word of God is *infallible* in total, *inerrant* in its parts, *complete* so that we are to add or subtract nothing, *authoritative* so that it is absolutely true and commands our obedience, *sufficient* so that it is able to do to us and for us everything we need, and *effective*—it will do exactly what it says it will do. Finally:

7. The Bible Is Determinative

The Bible is determinative because how you respond to the Word of God determines the essence of your life and your eternal destiny. In John 8:47 Jesus said, "He who is of God hears God's words; therefore you do not hear, because you are not of God." In other words, the determination of whether an individual is of God or not of God is based on whether he listens to the Word of God. First Corinthians 2:9 says, "Eye has not seen, nor ear heard, nor have entered into the heart of man the things which God has prepared for those who love Him." Man could never conceive of God's dominion on his own. Man could never conceive that he would be a part of it. Man could never conceive in his own humanness, in his own patterns of logic, all that God has prepared for him. But verses 10–12 say, "But God has revealed them to us through His Spirit. For the Spirit searches all things, yes, the deep things of God. For what man knows the things of a man except the spirit of the man which is in him? Even so no one knows the things of God except the Spirit of God. Now we have received, not the spirit of the world, but the Spirit who is from God, that we might know the things that have been freely given to us by

God." Then verse 14 says, "But the natural man does not receive the things of the Spirit of God."

There are two kinds of people: the people who receive the things of God, and the people who do not—the people who can receive, and the people who cannot. The unbelieving people can't receive it because they don't have the Holy Spirit. But the people who know God have the Holy Spirit, and they receive the Word of God. The Bible is the ultimate determiner. Those people who receive the Word of God indicate by their understanding of it that they possess the Holy Spirit—and that proves they are believers.

I remember talking to a man who continually admitted that he didn't understand the Bible. But he couldn't because he didn't have the one thing necessary to understand it—the indwelling of the Holy Spirit in his soul. So, the beauty, glory, and capabilities of the Word of God are presented to us in these simple words: it is *infallible, inerrant, complete, authoritative, sufficient, effective,* and *determinative*. Now somebody might come along and say, "Well, that's really great that the Bible makes all those claims for itself. If all of this is true then I've got to find out about those principles. But how can I really be sure that it's true?"

We live in a world where people really don't respond to authority very well. In fact, our whole world kicks against authority. We want to deny the authority of the home. There's a fight now to deny the authority of the man in our society. The women want to fight against that and maybe sometimes it has been oppressive. There often needs to be a little more balance, but it can be a fight against authority. Young people on junior high, high school, and college campuses sometimes fight against those in administration. There is sort of an antigovernment feeling in some cases. It's kind of rugged individualism; everybody's his own god. We're back to, "I'm the master of my fate. I'm the captain of my soul." We really don't like to respond to authority. So when you come along and say to somebody, "You know, I want to tell you the Bible is the absolute authority. It's absolutely sufficient and efficient," it comes across as harsh.

People respond with, "Well, how do I know that? I'm not going to accept that unless you can show me how." So how do we really determine that the Bible is true? Of course, ultimately you can't really prove it is true, but there certainly are some convincing things that make our faith sane.

The Authenticity of the Bible

There are five basic areas that prove that the Bible is true. The first area is:

1. Experience

I believe the Bible is true because it gives us the experience it claims it will give us. For example, Scripture says God will forgive our sin (1 John 1:9). I believe that. I accepted His forgiveness, and He granted it. But you may say, "How do you know that?" Because I have a sense of freedom from guilt; I have a sense of forgiveness. The Bible says that "if anyone is in Christ, he is a new creation; old things have passed away; behold, all things have become new" (2 Cor. 5:17). I came to Jesus Christ one day and experienced the passing away of old things and all things becoming new. The Bible changes lives. Someone said that a Bible that's falling apart usually belongs to somebody who isn't. That's true because the Bible can put lives together. Millions of people all over the world are living proof that the Bible is true. They've experienced it.

Although that's a great argument in one sense, it's a weak one in another sense, because if you start basing everything on experience, you're going to run into some people who have had some pretty wild experiences. Therefore if you base your proof all on human experience, you can encounter problems. So, experience is just one area of proof, and it's probably the weakest one, but it's still evidence for some.

A second thing that proves the validity of the Bible is:

2. Science

Some people say, "Well, the Bible is not a science book; it's scientifically incorrect, and it doesn't use scientific language. Why does the Old Testament say that the sun stood still? Now we know that the sun didn't stand still. In fact, in the old times they thought the sun was going around the earth instead of the other way around. That's just a typical biblical flaw." But what happened is that the earth stopped revolving, and it *appeared* that the sun stood still (Josh. 10:13). In trying to analyze the statement scientifically, people still see only what appeared to have happened. We all do that. When you get up in the morning and look toward the east, you don't say, "Oh my, what a lovely earth rotation." No, you call it a sunrise, and people understand what you're saying. Likewise, you don't look to the west and say, "What a lovely earth rotation." No, it's a sunset.

When someone asks you if you'd like another helping at dinner, you could say, "Well, gastronomical satiety admonishes me that I have arrived at a state of deglutition consistent with dietetic integrity." Or you could say, "No, thanks, I've had enough." You don't always need a scientific answer for everything. Sometimes just pure observation is sufficient. The Bible says some things from the viewpoint of human observation. But on the other hand, whenever the Bible speaks about a scientific principle, it is dead accurate. In fact, let's examine more closely three areas the Bible addresses.

The first is rainfall. In Isaiah 55:10 it says, "For as the rain comes down, and the snow from heaven, and do not return there, but water the earth, and make it bring forth and bud, that it may give seed to the sower, and bread to the eater." Isaiah spoke centuries before the hydrological cycle was ever discovered. He said, "The rain and the snow come down and don't return again until they have watered the earth." But it's only been in modern times that hydrology has been understood. This is what happens: the rain falls down on the land, it waters the land, it runs off into the streams, down to the rivers, into the sea, and from the sea it returns again to the clouds; then it is taken over the land and dropped again. The ever constant hydrological cycle, and Isaiah 55:10 laid it out.

Some might say, "Well, a blind pig can find the slop once in a while—maybe Isaiah just took a lucky guess." That might have been a possibility, but the Bible discusses the same information in several other portions. Job 36:27–29 comments, "For He draws up drops of water, which distill as rain from the mist, which the clouds drop down and pour abundantly on man. Indeed, can anyone understand the spreading of clouds, the thunder from His canopy?" Once again a discussion of rain.

Compare also what it says in Psalm 135:7: "He causes the vapors to ascend from the ends of the earth; He makes lightning for the rain; He brings the wind out of His treasuries." This is another wonderful mention of the sequence of rain and the ascending vapors from the sea to plant the water again in the clouds.

The fixed orbits of the heavenly bodies provide another scientific observation in Scripture. Jeremiah 31:35–36 (NASB) and Psalm 19 discuss this. I really feel that as you get into the Bible you will find incredible things about science that reveal the truthfulness of God's Word. You never need to be ashamed of the Bible. You're never going to run into a problem in the Bible that you can't solve in one of two ways: first, by looking through the rest of Scripture and understanding how to interpret it; second, by realizing that you're never going to understand it until you meet God. There are some things we don't understand or know, but we're not going to run into an error in the Scripture—not even scientifically.

A third scientific observation concerns balance. Within the science of geology there is a study called isostasy, which is fairly new. Isostasy is the study of the balance of the earth, and it says that equal weights are necessary to support equal weights. So, land mass must be supported equally by water mass. But scientists really haven't discovered anything new. If we go back again to

Isaiah, who was not a scientist but simply a prophet of God, we find this: "Who has measured the waters in the hollow of His hand, measured heaven with a span and calculated the dust of the earth in a measure? Weighed the mountains in scales and the hills in a balance?" (Isa. 40:12). God knew all about isostasy. It's just incredible when you come to the Bible and start to study it scientifically.

It was said of Herbert Spencer, who died in 1903, that he had discovered the greatest fact about the categorizing of all things in the universe. He said everything could fall into these five categories: time, force, action, space, and matter. The world hailed him as a great scientist, a great man of discovery. But all five of those categories are in the first verse of the Bible: "In the beginning (time) God (force) created (action) the heavens (space) and the earth (matter)." Genesis 1:1 shows us that when the Bible speaks, it speaks accurately. So, science is a good way to show the authority and validity of Scripture.

3. Christ

In addition to experience and science, another area of tremendous evidence for the truth of the Bible is the very life of Christ. *Jesus Himself believed in the authority of the Bible.* In Matthew 5:18 He says, "Till heaven and earth pass away, one jot or one tittle will by no means pass from the law till all is fulfilled." Furthermore, He showed His trust in the authority of Scripture by quoting from every part of the Old Testament. Jesus believed in the absolute, inspired authority of the Word of God.

4. Miracles

The fourth area of proof that the Bible is true is that of miracles. The Bible is a divine book because it includes miracles, and that proves that God is involved in it. It has to be a supernatural book because of all the supernatural activity it reports. Now some might say, "Well, how do you know all the miracles are true?" Because Scripture tells of miracles and provides supportive information. For example, when Jesus rose from the dead, more than five hundred people saw Him after the resurrection. Those are enough witnesses to convince any jury. The miraculous nature of the Bible speaks of God.

So experience, science, the testimony of Christ, and the miracles of the Bible all prove that Scripture is true. Yet there is one more compelling line of evidence.

5. Prophecy

There is no way to explain the Bible's prediction of historical events unless we see God as the Author. Peter Stoner, an expert in mathematical probabilities, wrote in his book *Science Speaks* that if you take just eight of the

Old Testament prophecies Christ fulfilled, and add up the probabilities that these eight prophecies could come to pass by accident, it would be one chance in 10^{17} that such an accident could happen—and yet every detail has come to pass. One chance in 10^{17} would be like filling the state of Texas two feet deep in silver dollars, putting an X on one of them, and giving a blind man one pick. He'd have one chance in 10^{17} of picking the one with an X on it. That's how much probability there is of these eight prophecies (with their specific details) ever coming to pass by accident. That's incredible! When the Bible speaks prophetically it is right, and it contains literally hundreds of fulfilled prophecies.

So we can look at experience, science, Christ, miracles, and fulfilled prophecy to see that the Bible is true. It's an incredible book—the greatest treasure imaginable.

The Bible is God's holy Word; it's a tremendous resource. But the Christian who never approaches it with an intense commitment to study it is forfeiting a tremendous blessing.

Bible scholar Donald G. Barnhouse was once traveling by air and reading the book of Romans. You might think he was the last man on the earth who needed to read the book of Romans because he wrote volumes on the book. But he was reading Romans and there was a seminary student sitting next to him on the plane. The student was reading *Time* magazine and kept looking up from his magazine and staring over because he kept thinking he recognized this man. Finally, the student asked him, "Sir, I don"t want to interrupt you but aren't you Dr. Donald Barnhouse?"

When Dr. Barnhouse responded yes, the student shared, "Dr. Barnhouse, you're such a fabulous teacher of the Scripture. I wish that I could know the Bible like you do."

Dr. Barnhouse looked at him and said, "Well you could start by putting down *Time* magazine and reading the Bible." That sounds like a hard shot, but he's right.

I think about the great Bible teacher who had a young man come up to him and say, "Oh sir, I'd give the world if I knew the Bible like you." The Bible teacher looked him right in the eye and said, "Good, because that's exactly what it will cost you." You must realize what a precious gift the Bible is. This is the treasure of God. It can do what you need done in your life. To walk away from it is incredible.

THE BENEFITS OF
STUDYING GOD'S WORD

I want to give you six areas that appear as major bene-fits, because these are the things that are going to become your motivation. I'll provide the first two to conclude this chapter and present the remaining four in our next chapter.

BENEFIT ONE: The Source of Truth

In John 17:17b Jesus prayed to the Father and said, "Your word is truth." That's a great statement, but do you realize what it is to have the truth? Quite often when I confront people about Jesus Christ they say, "But I don't know what the truth is." Even Pilate came to the place in his life when he looked at Jesus and said, "What is truth?" (John 18:38a). Many people have that same thought; nevertheless, we're in a world that searches for truth.

By the 1980s people printed nearly three thousand new pages of information every sixty seconds. Yet today's digital age produces more content than any organization can accurately count. One thing is certain—our society is chasing truth.

The Bible even says that humans are "always learning and never able to come to the knowledge of the truth" (2 Tim. 3:7). Do you know what that's like? I remember when I was in junior high school, I had a terrible time with algebra. I'd go home and work on one of those silly problems for hours. Then I'd go back to school the next day without the answer, and that was so frustrating to me. But you've had that problem too: you've worked on something and never solved it or found the answer. And that's the way it is with people in the world. They read, they study, they think, they reason, they listen, they talk, they interact, and they never get the real truth. They never settle on anything, and the frustration is overwhelming.

I remember talking to a man who just kind of left society altogether; he just bailed out and got on drugs. He had graduated from Boston University but was living in the woods, sleeping in a small tent. I asked him, "What made you do this?"

He said, "Well, I searched for the answer so long, I finally decided to blow my mind on drugs. At least now I don't even have to ask the questions." Now that's the despair of never knowing the truth.

The writer Franz Kafka gave a great illustration about education. He pictured a bombed-out city consisting only of rubble. Everywhere there were people bleeding and dying; there was smoke and smoldering fire—just total rubble. But in the middle of the city was an ivory tower piercing the sky, pristine white, untouched by any bombs. Then, there was a solitary figure winding his way through the rubble. When he got to the tall white building, he walked in and went up to the top story. He came to a dark hall, and at the end of it was a little light. He walked in the darkness until he came to the light, turned, and walked into a bathroom. Inside sat a man with a fishing pole fishing in the bathtub. The solitary stranger said to him. "Hey, what are you doing?"

The man said, "I'm fishing."

The stranger looked in the bathtub and said, "There are no fish in the bathtub and there is no water."

The man said. "I know," and kept on fishing.

Kafka said, "That is *higher education.*"

You see, man has lost the truth.

It's fantastic to realize—and sometimes I think we forget it—that every time we pick up the Bible, we pick up the truth. What a tremendous legacy we have. But we can't take it for granted, and we certainly can't let it just sit around. So the first reason I believe we need to study the Word of God is that it's the source of truth. Jesus said, "If you abide in my word . . . you shall know the truth, and the truth shall make you free" (John 8:31b–32). What did He mean by that? Like the man who works on a math problem and finds the answer—he's free. Just like the scientist in the lab pouring the different solutions into test tubes, he stays with it until he says, "Eureka, I found it!"—then he's free. Humanity will search and struggle and grapple and grope for the truth until it finds it—then people are genuinely free.

One reason to study the Bible is that the truth is there. The truth about God; the truth about man; the truth about life; the truth about death; the truth about you and me; the truth about men, women, children, husbands, wives, dads, and mothers; the truth about friends and enemies; the truth about how you ought to be at work and how you ought to be at home; even the truth about how you ought to eat and drink, how you ought to live, how you ought to think—the truth is all there. What a resource we have. Cherish it.

BENEFIT TWO: The Source of Happiness

A second reason you should want to study the Bible is it's the source of happiness. Some would rather use "joy" or "blessing," but "happiness" says it. The truth is there and it brings us happiness. In Psalm 19:8a it says, "The statutes of the Lord are right, rejoicing the heart." It's just talking about the principles of the Scripture. When you begin to study the Bible and learn the great truths it contains, you will get excited. I study the Bible a lot because I'm constantly teaching and preaching the Word, but I also study it on my own because I love it so much, and the exhilaration that comes to me in the discovery of great truths in the Word of God has never diminished. The greatest thrill I've known in my life is the tremendous exhilaration that comes to my heart when I have cracked open the shell of an incredible truth in the Word of God. In fact, Proverbs 8:34 says, "Blessed [happy] is the man who listens to me," In Luke 11:28 Jesus says, "Blessed [happy] are those who hear the word of God and keep it!" Do you want to be a happy person? Then obey God's Word.

It's amazing to me how so many people know what the Bible teaches, but they don't obey it—so they forfeit happiness. Some people say, "Well, the book of Revelation is so hard to understand. I study the other stuff, but I don't want to get involved in Revelation." But look at what Revelation 1:3 says: "Blessed is he who reads and those who hear the words of this prophecy." The word "blessed" means "happy." Do you want to be happy? Read Revelation. Yes, to be happy, read the Word of God and respond to it. I love 1 John 1:4 that says, "And these things we write to you that your joy may be full."

Then there's a wonderful statement made by our Lord in that magnificent fifteenth chapter of John in which He presents Himself as the Vine. In verse 11 He says, "These things I have I spoken to you, that My joy may remain in you, and that your joy may be full." What a tremendous thought—joy from the Scripture.

In Luke 24 Jesus has risen from the dead and He is on His way to Emmaus with the two disciples who don't recognize Him (vv. 13–32). Beginning in verse 24 they tell Jesus, "And certain of those who were with us went to the tomb and found it just as the women had said: but Him they did not see. Then he said to them, 'O foolish ones, and slow of heart to believe in all that the prophets have spoken!'" Christ is talking to them, but they don't know who He is. "Ought not the Christ to have suffered these things and to enter into His glory?" After His resurrection, nobody knew who Christ was until He revealed Himself to them. "And beginning at Moses and all the Prophets, he expounded to them in all the Scriptures the things concerning Himself." Jesus taught them through the Scriptures, and they were listening. Then as they had their meal, all of a sudden the light dawned: "Then their eyes were opened and they knew Him; and He vanished from their sight." Then I love this, "And they said to one another, 'Did not our heart burn within us while He talked with us on the road, and while He opened the Scriptures to us?'" When He opened the Scriptures to them, their hearts virtually burned within them.

There is joy in the Word of God if you obey it. If you don't keep His Word, then there's no joy. However, I would also add that God is gracious. He doesn't expect us to be able to keep every single principle all the time and never waver, but it is a matter of heart attitude. If your heart is committed to obeying the Word, then He'll fill your life with joy. I know people want to know truth and they want to be happy, especially those of us who are Christians. Thus there is no excuse for us not knowing the truth and not living lives that are filled with exhilaration and joy—we have it available right in the Word of God.

Review

1. Why is the Bible the only Book for a living man as well as a dying man?

2. How can we know that the Bible is infallible in its original autographs?

3. What word describes that the Bible is true in its parts?

4. What passage of the Bible is a testimony to its completeness?

5. Why does the Bible demand obedience?

6. Give some verses that support the authority of the Bible.

7. What things is the Bible sufficient for? Explain.

8. What is Scripture profitable for? Explain (2 Tim. 3:16).

9. According to James 1:21, what is the Word of God able to do when you receive it?

10. What does Isaiah 55:11 indicate about the Bible?

11. Explain how the Bible is determinative. How are believers able to understand the Word of God? Why can't unbelievers understand it (1 Cor. 2:9–14)?

12. Explain how experience is able to prove that the Bible is true. What is the weakness in using experience as proof ?

13. What are three areas of science that the Bible discusses?

14. How does the Bible support the scientific principle of hydrology (Isa. 55:10)?

15. What is the study of isostasy? What does the Bible say about it (Isa. 40:12)?

16. What five classic scientific categories are found in the first verse of the Bible?

17. How did Jesus Christ reveal His trust in the authority of Scripture?

18. How can we know that all the miracles recorded in the Bible are true?

19. What is the only way to explain how the Bible could predict historical events accurately?

20. What verse in the Bible indicates that God's Word is the source of truth?

21. What did Jesus mean when He said, "If you abide in my word . . . you shall know the truth, and the truth shall make you free" (John 8:31–32)?

22. What are some of the truths that are found in the Bible?

23. Since the Bible is the source of truth, what does it give to the one who believes it (Ps. 19:8)?

24. How can you be a happy person?

Reflect

1. Read 2 Timothy 3:16–17. In what ways has the Bible been profitable to you in teaching you doctrine? In what ways have others used Scripture to reprove you? In what ways have others used it to correct your spiritual walk? How have others used the Bible to train you in righteousness? Just as others have had the opportunity to use the Bible to move you along the path of perfection, look for opportunities to be used of God in the same way in another person's life.

2. Read 1 Corinthians 2:9–12. How are Christians able to know spiritual truth? Take this time to thank God for your salvation, and that because of your salvation you can learn spiritual truth. Ask Him to give you greater insight into His Word. But just as you want to learn more from Him, He wants a greater commitment on your part to study

His Word. Make that commitment by setting aside a specific time each day to study God's Word.

3. Read Psalm 19:7–11. According to those verses, what are the benefits of God's Word? In what ways has each of those benefits been manifest in your life? Be specific. How desirous are you of studying God's Word? According to verse 11, what is the result of obeying God's Word? As a result of this study, how has your attitude changed regarding your Bible study? What changes will you implement to get more out of your study?

2

THE POWER
of the WORD in the BELIEVER'S LIFE
Part 2

In our previous chapter, we said that we should study the Bible because it is the source of truth and the source of happiness. Jesus, in Luke 11:28, says, "Blessed [happy] are those who hear the word of God and keep it!" When we talk about obeying the Word of God we need to differentiate between two kinds of obedience: first, legal obedience, and second, gracious obedience.

Legal obedience, or we could better call it legalistic obedience, pertains to the "covenant of works," the "old covenant," or the "Mosaic covenant." Legalistic obedience demands absolute, perfect obedience without a single failure (Gal. 3:10). If you fail, that's the end. One false move and you're finished. This is the "covenant of works," but in contrast to that, God gives us the "covenant of grace."

Gracious obedience pertains to God's loving, gracious, merciful, and forgiving attitude. Legalistic obedience says you had better keep every rule or you're finished. Gracious obedience says if God sees in your heart a spirit of grace; if He sees a sincere and loving and humble willingness to obey; if He sees a positive response to His Word—even though there are times when we fail—then He counts us as obedient. Even though our gracious obedience may be filled with defects, it's the proper attitude that God is after. That's a tremendous principle, and I want to illustrate it for you.

A favorite chapter of mine, John 21, vividly illustrates several spiritual truths. It's all about Peter, who had gone fishing when he shouldn't have. The Lord had already called him into the ministry, but when he and other disciples went fishing and violated the Lord's call, they caught nothing. When morning came, Jesus appeared on the shore and asked them if they had caught anything. Peter, like the rest, had nothing to show. It was a great lesson for them because God was saying, "If you think you can go back to fishing, you're wrong. You've been called to the ministry, so your fishing is finished. I can reroute every fish in every sea you approach." So Jesus called them over for breakfast.

The Lord had made breakfast, and I imagine He made breakfast like He made anything: "Breakfast!"—and there it was. After they had eaten, verse 15 says, "Jesus said to Simon Peter, 'Simon, son of Jonah, do you love me more than these?'" That was an interesting statement. Jesus used the most grandiose word for "love" in the Greek language, *agapaō* from which we get the word *agapē*.

In other words, Jesus said, "Do you super love Me? Do you love Me to the limit of love?" Peter responded, "I sure like You a lot." Peter used a different word that spoke of a lesser love, *phileō*. And the Lord said, "Feed My lambs." The second time Jesus said to Peter, "Peter, do you super love Me?" Peter replied, "Well Lord, I like You a lot." Jesus said, "Tend my sheep" (v. 16). Do you know why Peter kept saying, "I like You a lot," instead of using the word for love that Jesus used? Simple. His life didn't match such a claim. He knew if he said, "Lord, I super love You," Jesus would have said, "Oh, is that why you don't obey? Have you forgotten that I told you a long time ago that if you love Me you'll keep My commandments? How could you say you super love Me when you don't even do what I say?" Peter wasn't about to get himself into that trap, so he said, "I like You a lot."

"He said to him the third time, 'Simon, son of Jonah,

do you love me?" (v. 17). Jesus said, "Peter, do you like Me a lot?" Now that hurt. Peter thought he was being fair; he wasn't even going to claim super love, but Jesus questioned the love that Peter did claim. The verse continues, "Peter was grieved because He said to him the third time, 'Do you love me?' [Do you like Me a lot?] And he said to Him, 'Lord, You know all things; You know that I love You.'" Peter said, "Lord, You know everything, You know I like You a lot" (NASB).

He appealed to the doctrine of omniscience. He wanted Jesus to read his heart because his love wasn't obvious from his life. The doctrine of omniscience is a great reality, but when I was a kid I thought it was bad; I thought God was going around spying on everybody. Now I realize that if God weren't omniscient there would be plenty of days He wouldn't know I loved Him because it wouldn't be obvious from my life. So Peter says, "Lord, You know everything—You know that I love You."

And do you know what the Lord Jesus told Peter? He looked at that disciple who couldn't even claim the supreme love—that one who couldn't even obey, that one who couldn't even stay awake at a prayer meeting, that one who stuck his foot in his mouth every time he had an opportunity, that one who almost drowned when he could have walked on water, that one who wanted to tell Jesus not to go to the cross, that one who grabbed a sword and tried to chop up the Roman army—and Jesus said to that apostle who had fouled up so many opportunities, "You're My man." Three times He said, "Feed my lambs . . . feed my sheep . . . feed my sheep" (vv. 15–17 KJV).

Jesus took Peter on the basis of his heart attitude of willingness to obey, even though he blundered. God works with us on the premise of gracious obedience—not legal obedience. Here was a man who failed to obey over and over again, but in his heart he really wanted to do it. The spirit was willing, but the flesh was weak. The Lord Jesus knew that, and that's how God looks at us. He says, "My Word is the source of joy if you obey it, and if you obey My Word, I'll fill your life with joy." No, He doesn't mean that if you ever fail one little bit in His rules, that's the end of joy and the start of misery. Instead, He says, "If I read as an attitude of your heart a style of life that shows a commitment and the desire to obey, I will pass over those failures." It's the deep commitment He's after, and that's the source of joy.

As you study the Word and hear what it says, and you draw out its principles and obey those principles because it's in your heart to obey them, then God pours out the blessing and joy. But if you crank out obedience in every legalistic manner possible and in your heart you don't want to obey, He will never give you the joy. To do good deeds without the right heart attitude doesn't count.

Let me show you what I mean. The Bible talks about different kinds of fruit, and it talks about the fruit of the Spirit. Before there's ever fruit in your life, such as winning people to Christ, and before the fruit on the outside means anything, it has to come from the fruit of the Spirit on the inside. Action fruit, things you do without the proper attitude, is pure legalism—Pharisaism without joy. On the other hand, if you have a heart of obedience with the right attitude, even though you may fail on the outside, God will give you joy because He sees the gracious, obedient spirit in your heart. That's what He desires.

One thing we must realize is that God doesn't tell us exactly when we're going to get the joy—we might have to wait a little while. In John 16 Jesus said to the disciples, "I'm leaving" (v. 16). They just sat there moping because everybody had left his job and had been following Jesus for three years. Then Jesus said, "One day soon I'm going to leave" (v. 17 paraphrase). They all thought, *Now wait a minute—we joined this endeavor thinking the kingdom was going to come. What's wrong?* They were very sorrowful, so Jesus said, "Most assuredly, I say to you that you will weep and lament, but the world will rejoice; and you will be sorrowful, but your sorrow will be turned to joy" (John 16:20). In other words, "You've got to realize that sometimes there's going to be sorrow before there's ever going to be joy." In fact, if we didn't know sorrow, we wouldn't understand joy when it came. If we didn't know pain, we wouldn't know pleasure.

I once read an interesting article that said the difference between an itch and a tickle cannot be defined medically. Yet, a tickle is something that makes you happy, and an itch is something that irritates. The difference between pleasure and pain can be a very fine line. For example, sometimes there's nothing more wonderful than a real hot shower, but you have to ease in because of the pain: then all of a sudden—ahhh!—the thin line between pain and pleasure. If we didn't know pain we wouldn't know the joy that pleasure could bring.

I played football when I was in college. All through college I faced that thin line between pain and pleasure. You torture your body like some kind of maniac and you're in pain. Yet all that time you love it with some kind of perverse pleasure.

Again, I think one of the reasons God allows sorrow in our lives is so we will understand joy when it comes. If we obey the Word of God, He'll give us that joy. Maybe not instantaneously when we want it, but always when we need it. No matter what happens in my life, externally and circumstantially, when I study the Word of God there's an exhilaration and a joy that is untouched by any circumstance.

So, why should we study the Bible? In our previous chapter, we learned that first, it's the source of truth. Second, it's the source of rejoicing. But those aren't the only benefits. And we must understand those benefits apart from legal obedience.

BENEFIT THREE: The Source of Victory

A third motivating force, and the third reason to study the Bible, is that the Word is the source of victory. I lose a lot, but I don't like it. I figure if you're going to do something, do it all the way with the goal of winning. My dad used to say to me from the time I was young, "Listen, Johnny, if you're going to do it, do it to the best of your ability, or it isn't worth doing." I grew up that way, striving for excellence.

I also see this in my Christian life. I don't like to give an occasion to the adversary. I don't like to give him an advantage over me, as it says in 2 Corinthians 2:11. I don't like to see Satan victorious; I don't like to see the world master me; I don't like to see the flesh override my spirit—I want to win.

I remember my football coach giving us the typical Knute Rockne (the legendary University of Notre Dame football coach of the 1920s) lecture saying, "You can't be beat, if you won't be beat." We ought to think like that as

Christians. There's no reason to give in to the enemy, because as you study the Bible, you'll find out that the Word of God becomes the source of victory.

We would do well to remember what David said: "Your word I have hidden in my heart, that I might not sin against You" (Ps. 119:11). The Word, then, is the source of victory over sin. As the Word of God is taken in, it becomes the resource the Holy Spirit uses to direct us. We have no way of preventing ourselves from being led into sin, unless we can bring the Word of God into our conscious minds. Let me give you something basic to understand: We'll never function on what we don't know. We'll never be able to apply a truth or principle we haven't discovered. So as we feed into our minds the Word of God, it becomes the resource by which the Spirit of God directs and guides. Now let's look at some specific examples of the Word's effectiveness.

Victory over Satan (Matt. 4:1–11)

Matthew 4 provides a classic illustration of facing Satan with the Word of God. It says in verse 1, "Then Jesus was led up by the Spirit into the wilderness to be tempted by the devil." The Greek word *peirasmos* can mean either "temptation" or "testing." It's a neutral word that can connate good or bad. From Satan's viewpoint, he wanted it to be bad; from God's viewpoint, He knew it would be good. So the Holy Spirit led Him into the wilderness knowing He'd pass the test, but Satan was there waiting for Him, hoping He'd fail.

In verse 2 we read, "And when He had fasted forty days and forty nights, afterward He was hungry." That's not surprising, but it's interesting as we remember that Jesus was a perfect human being, without sin; therefore, His body must have had powers beyond anything we could ever experience. It's really amazing to realize that He did not feel the gnawing pangs of hunger until the end of those forty days.

At that time, "When the tempter came to Him, he said, 'If You are the Son of God, command that these stones become bread.'" What Satan's really saying to Jesus is this: "Listen, You're the Son of God. You deserve better than this. What are You doing out here in this wretched wilderness? What are You doing out here starving to death? You're the Son of God, grab some satisfaction, make some bread. You deserve it." The devil was really tempting Him to go against God's plan—to grab His own satisfaction. He was saying, "Do Your own thing—don't depend on God; He hasn't met Your need."

Satan was tempting Jesus to distrust the care of God. "But He answered and said, 'It is written, "Man shall not live by bread alone, but by every word that proceeds out of the mouth of God."'" The Lord quoted Deuteronomy

8:3. In other words, He said, "God promised to care for Me, so I'll keep My trust in that promise, and I'll never use My own powers to violate the promise of God." Jesus countered Satan's temptation with the Word of God.

In verse 5 we read, "Then the devil took Him up into the holy city (Jerusalem), set Him on a pinnacle of the temple." This was probably the strut that protruded over the Valley of Hinnom and was 300 feet above the ground. Satan said, "Throw Yourself down." Then he quoted Scripture: "'He shall give His angels charge over you,' and 'In their hands they shall bear you up, lest you dash your foot against a stone.'" He said, "If You want to trust God, if You're going to believe God, well, why don't You really believe God and take a swan dive off here and see if He fulfills His Word?"

However, "Jesus said to him, 'It is written again, "You shall not tempt the Lord your God'" (v. 7). In other words, "You don't presume on God." When you believe Him to care for you on a trip, you don't lie in the freeway. There's a big difference between trust and presumption.

Satan then took Jesus to a high mountain and showed Him the kingdoms of the world. He said, "'All these things will I give You, if You will fall down and worship me.' Then Jesus said to him, 'Away with you, Satan! For it is written, "You shall worship the Lord your God, and Him only shall you serve.'" Then the devil left Him,

and behold, angels came and ministered to Him" (vv. 9–
11). God fulfilled all His promises.

The point is this: Jesus answered the temptation of
Satan three times, and every time He quoted directly out
of the Old Testament. As Christians, it is the capturing of
biblical truth in our consciousness that enables us to defeat Satan. We can't do it on our own. Jesus triumphed
over the devil through the Word of God—it is the source
of victory. But it's just incredible that people still imagine
they can argue Satan out of temptation through their own
logic. It can't be done. Only God's Word gives us victory.

Victory over Demons (Luke 4:33–36)

Luke 4 provides another interesting illustration, beginning in verse 33: "Now in the synagogue there was a
man who had a spirit of an unclean demon. And he cried
out with a loud voice, saying, 'Let us alone! What have
we to do with You, Jesus of Nazareth? Did You come to
destroy us? I know who You are—the Holy One of God!'
But Jesus rebuked him, saying, 'Be quiet, and come out
of him!'" And when the demon had thrown him in their
midst, it came out of him and did not hurt him. Then
they were all amazed and spoke among themselves, saying, 'What a word this is! For with authority and power
he commands the unclean spirits, and they come out.'"

Jesus once again established His authority and power

over Satan with His Word. With one word He vanquished a legion of demons. The people recognized that Jesus spoke as a man of authority, not like the scribes and the Pharisees. The Word of Jesus Christ is absolutely authoritative. So, when you know the Word of God, you'll know victory.

Victory over Temptation (Eph. 6:17)

In Ephesians 6—Paul's discussion of the armor of the Christian—we find that it finishes with a great piece of armor: "And take the helmet of salvation, and the sword of the Spirit, which is the word of God" (v. 17). He says the final piece of armor is "the sword of the Spirit, which is the word of God." When we think of a sword, we usually think of a long blade that someone flails around. The Greek word for that type of sword is *rhomphaia*. But the Greek word used here is *machaira*, which refers to a short, small dagger. The sword of the Spirit, therefore, is not a huge sword that you just flail around, hoping that you'll whack off the head of a demon sooner or later. It is not something you use indiscriminately or wildly. Instead, the sword of the Spirit is a *machaira*—it is a dagger; it is incisive; it must hit a vulnerable spot or it doesn't do any damage. The sword of the Spirit is not something general, but a very specific spiritual weapon.

Furthermore, the Greek word used for "word" in this

verse is not *logos*. *Logos* is a general word: the Bible is the *logos*; Christ is the *logos*; or a general "word" is *logos*. When the New Testament wants to speak of a specific, it uses the word *rhema*. Here it means "a specific statement." So the sword of the Spirit is the specific statement of the Word of God that meets the specific point of temptation. Some people may say, "Well, I have the sword of the Spirit—I own a Bible." But you could own a Bible warehouse and still not have the sword of the Spirit.

Having the sword of the Spirit is not owning a Bible, but knowing the specific principle in the Bible that applies to the specific point of temptation. The only way Christians will know victory in the Christian life is to know the principles of the Word of God so they can apply them to the specific points where Satan, the world, and the flesh attack. As Christians fill themselves with the Word of God, it then becomes the source of victory. We can't live the Christian life without studying the Bible. It's the source of truth, it's the source of joy, and it's the source of victory.

BENEFIT FOUR: The Source of Growth

The Word of God is also beneficial as the source of growth. It is a sad thing to see Christians who don't grow spiritually. The reason they don't grow is because they really don't study the Word. They may go to church, but when they go they take a thimble, fill it up, and spill it on the steps as they're leaving. Nothing ever happens, and that's sad. Peter said in 1 Peter 2:2, "As newborn babes, desire the pure milk of the word, that you may grow thereby." In other words, the Word of God is the source of growth.

When I was a younger Christian and in college, I was involved in all sorts of activities, so I didn't grow much. However, when I got to seminary and got a taste of the Word of God, I found I had such a desire for the Word that I could hardly stand the longing. I had this tremendous desire to grow, and I realized there was only one way it was going to happen—I had to study the Word of God. My growth, then, was directly proportionate to the amount of time and effort I spent in the study of Scripture.

Let's look at some specifics concerning this growth.

Prerequisites for Growth

A first prerequisite for growth is sanctification. In 1 Peter 2:1 it is interesting to see how we must first lay some groundwork: "Therefore, laying aside all malice [Gk., *kakia*, 'general evil'], all deceit [the same Greek word is also used for 'fishhook'], hypocrisy, envy, and all evil speaking." In other words, we must set aside all evil things, confess our sin, get our life straightened out, and hit the Word with a tremendous desire—then we begin to grow. The more we grow, the more exciting it becomes. The Word is a source of life that helps us mature and grow stronger; then we are able to defeat Satan, and we come to know more about God and His character. We are enriched in every possible way.

In addition, we must study. In John 6:63b Jesus says, "The words that I speak to you are spirit, and they are life." Jeremiah said, "Your words were found, and I ate them" (15:16a). That's feeding on the Word of God! James 1:18a says, "Of His own will He brought us forth by the word of truth." The Word is a life-giver, a life-sustainer, and a life-builder. It is tremendous nourishment. First Timothy 4:6 states, "If you instruct the brethren in these things, you will be a good minister of Jesus Christ, nourished in the words of faith." Therefore, the Word nourishes us, feeds us, builds us, and causes us to grow.

Patterns of Growth (1 John 2:13–14)

God wants us mature; He wants us built up; He wants us strong. In 1 John 2:13 we find the pattern of growth: "I write to you, fathers, because you have known Him who is from the beginning. I write unto you, young men, because you have overcome the wicked one. I write to you, little children, because you have known the Father." Those are three categories of spiritual growth—they are not literally little children, young men, and fathers. It's talking about three *levels* of spiritual growth.

We all start out as little children—we know the Father. That's spiritual "Da-Da." You don't know much when you're a new Christian, but you know "Jesus loves me, this I know, for the Bible tells me so." You realize God is your Father and it's great, but you're not very mature spiritually. So you don't want to stay there; that would be sad. You need go to the second level.

What is the characteristic of a young man? He has overcome—past tense—the wicked one. Who is the wicked one? Satan. "Are you telling me that I could reach the point in my life where I actually overcome Satan?" That's right.

How? Verse 14 says, "I have written to you, fathers, because you have known Him who is from the beginning. I have written to you, young men, because you are strong, and the word of God abides in you, and you have overcome the wicked one." To overcome Satan you have to be strong, and there's only one way—that's to have the Word abiding in you. Do you know what a spiritual young man is? He's someone who really knows the Word.

Here's why I say that. Satan, according to 2 Corinthians 11:14, comes disguised as an angel of light. I believe he spends 99 percent of his time in false religious systems.

I believe the problems we have with bars, prostitution, crime, the lust of the world, and all the rest of that evil is pretty well taken care of by the flesh. Galatians 5:19–21 lists the works of the flesh. I don't think Satan is running around nagging us about every little sin; I believe he is developing worldwide systems of evil. The devil is appearing as an angel of light, and his demonic ministers are angels of light as he works in false religions.

A spiritual young man is somebody who overcomes Satan because he knows enough about the Word of God that he is not enticed by false religion. Rather, he is angered by it. For example, the characteristic of a spiritual child, according to Ephesians 4:14, is that he is "tossed to and fro and carried about with every wind of doctrine." Spiritual babies have trouble with false doctrine. Spiritual young men are people who know their Bible. They know their doctrine, so false doctrine from Satan doesn't appeal to them at all.

In verse 13a John says, "I write to you, fathers, because you have known Him who is from the beginning." Do you know who the fathers are? They are the ones who have gone beyond the page. They don't just know the doctrine—fathers have a deep knowledge of the God behind the doctrine.

In these three steps we have the progress of spiritual growth. We start out as babies, and as we feed on the

Word of God, we become strong. We never totally overcome the flesh, but we can overcome the world; our faith does that (1 John 5:4). The flesh will always be a problem, but we can have the joy of overcoming Satan's false systems of religion. I can tell every time men or women get to the place of being spiritual young people. They invariably get to the place where false religion makes them angry, so they want to speak out about false religious movements. Then as they mature, they're not so concerned with fighting alternative religions—they begin to get a taste of who God is. They begin to plumb the depths of the mind of the eternal God and stretch toward being a spiritual father, walking in the presence of the Holy One. That's where we ought to go in our growth.

You cheat yourself if you stay a baby. You cheat yourself if you stay a spiritual young man and all you know is doctrine. You must strive to reach the place where you begin to walk in the very presence of the God of the universe, where you really begin to touch the Person Himself. That's the ultimate end of growth.

BENEFIT FIVE: The Source of Power

We must study the Word of God because it is the source of power. It is the Word of God that infuses us with spiritual power, but there's nothing worse than feeling like a powerless Christian. In Acts 1:8a we read, "But you shall receive power." The Greek word for "power" is *dunamis*, which means "miraculous power" (it is the source of our word "dynamite"). Thus someone might say we ought to be exploding all over the world with this tremendous power. But you say to yourself, "Exploding!? I don't even fizzle! I feel like a dud." Someone else might say we ought to be out there winning people to Jesus Christ. But you say, "Are you kidding? Not me. I'm like Moses, I—I—I can't talk" (see Ex. 3:10).

Sometimes we get hung up by our inabilities because we really don't know the power available to us. The Word of God will infuse us with power. From my own life I've realized that the more I know about the Word of God, the less I fear any situation, because the Word is my resource. In fact, let's look at various Scriptures to see how the Bible is a resource for power.

Hebrews 4:12: "For the word of God is living and powerful, and sharper than any two-edged sword, piercing even to the division of soul and spirit, and of joints and marrow, and is a discerner of the thoughts and intents of the heart." When you pick up the Bible and read it, it will cut to the very depths of your being. The Bible is a powerful book!

Romans 1:16: The apostle Paul said, "For I am not

ashamed of the gospel of Christ, for it is the power of God to salvation for everyone who believes." When you share the gospel with someone, you can see its power as it crumbles every bit of false philosophy built up over the years.

Ephesians 4:23: "And be renewed in the spirit of your mind." Our thinking will change.

Romans 12:2: "But be transformed by the renewing of your mind." There's a life-changing transformation.

2 Corinthians 3:18: "But we all, with unveiled face, beholding as in a mirror the glory of the Lord, are being transformed into the same image from glory to glory, just as by the Spirit of the Lord." As we focus on the Word of God, the power it will have in our lives is incredible. As we meditate on it, it empowers us. It's like the old computer saying, "G.I.G.O., garbage in—garbage out." Whatever we pump into our computers is just what's going to come regurgitating out in our lives. As we feed on the Word of God, it's going to come right back out in our lives. It's our source of energy.

Ephesians 1:3–3:20: In the first three chapters of Ephesians the apostle Paul lists several things he wants us to know. They are full of theology and contain some great truths:

"God . . . who has blessed us with every spiritual blessing in the heavenly places in Christ" (1:3b).

"He made us accepted in the Beloved" (1:6)

"In Him we have redemption" (1:7a).

"In Him we have . . . the forgiveness of sins" (1:7b).

We've been given "all wisdom and prudence" (1:8).

We've been given the knowledge of the ages to know the eternal plan of God (1:9–10).

We've been "sealed with the Holy Spirit of promise" (1:13).

We have the Holy Spirit "who is the guarantee of our inheritance" (1:14).

Christ has "broken down the middle wall of separation" (2:14).

We have come together "to God in one body through the cross" (2:16).

We are "fellow citizens with the saints and members of the household of God" (2:19).

We are "being built together for a dwelling place of God in the Spirit" (2:22).

We have "the unsearchable riches of Christ" (3:8).

We have been made to "see what is the fellowship of the mystery, which . . . has been hidden in God" (3:9).

All these incredible riches are ours, and Paul wants us to know them. He says in 1:17–18 that he prayed that God would "give to you the spirit of wisdom and revelation in the knowledge of Him, the eyes of your understanding being enlightened; that you may know . . . what are the riches of the glory of His inheritance in the saints." So he said if you would learn these truths, then you would realize the truth of what he says in 3:20— "Now to Him who is able to do exceedingly abundantly above all that we ask or think, according to the power that works in us." Do you see the resources? Did you ever think about the fact that you can do everything you can think? Did you ever think about the fact that you can do above everything you can think? Did you ever think about the fact that you can do exceedingly, abundantly above all you can ask or think? That's a lot of power, isn't it? Frankly, there's no sense flopping around on one cylinder when you have those kinds of resources. As you feed on the Word of God, it has a powerful effect. It makes your life an energy source that can confront anybody, anytime, with the truth.

So we're to study the Word of God because it is the source of truth, the source of happiness, the source of victory, the source of growth, and the source of power. Yet there is one more key benefit to the study of God's Word.

BENEFIT SIX: The Source of Guidance

We are to study the Bible because it is also the source of guidance. Whenever I want to know what God wants me to do, I go to the Word. You hear people say, "I'm searching for the will of God." Is God's will *lost?* They think God is the celestial Easter bunny who stashes His will in earth's bushes and then sits in heaven telling believers, "You're getting warmer," or, "You're getting colder." That isn't true. God's will is easy to find; it's right in His book. When we study the Bible, we find over and over again the phrase, "This is the will of God."

Therefore we can know the will of God by studying the Word of God. What does Psalm 119:105 say? "Your word is a lamp to my feet and a light to my path." That's pretty simple—the Word is a guide. If I have a decision to make, I find the place in the Bible where possibly someone in the Old or New Testament grappled with a similar decision. I try to see how God led them. Or I'll go to a text in the Bible that gives me a direct answer.

But there's a subjective element here also: as Christians we have the Holy Spirit (Rom. 8:9). First John 2:27 says, "But the anointing which you have received from Him abides in you, and you do not need that anyone teach you; but as the same anointing teaches you concerning all things." When you study the Bible, the Holy

Spirit in you takes the Word of God and makes a personal application that will give you guidance. That's an incredible combination—to have the truth and the resident truth teacher. It's that combination that guides the believer. What have we learned? There are great benefits to studying the Bible. It is the source of truth, happiness, victory, growth, power, and guidance.

If this is really true, if the Bible is going to do all these things, then how should we respond? Let me provide a few applications to consider.

1. Believe It

If the Bible says it—believe it. Jesus said to the Twelve one time, "'Do you also want to go away?' But Simon Peter answered Him, 'Lord, to whom shall we go? You have the words of eternal life'" (John 6:67–68). Peter said, "You can't get rid of me. I found the source of truth." If God's Word is true, then hang in there—believe it.

2. Honor It

If this is the Word of God, then honor it. In Job 23:12b there is that magnificent statement of Job when he says, "I have treasured the words of His mouth more than my necessary food." If the Bible is the Word of God—and it will do everything we just said it would do—then believe it and honor it. In fact, in Psalm

138:2b, the psalmist says, "for You have magnified Your word above all Your name." Isn't that incredible? God honors the Word.

In Ephesus, the citizens worshiped the goddess Diana. People think of Diana as some stylish, beautiful young woman. But she was an ugly, dark beast that was one of the most grotesque-looking creatures ever seen. But they worshiped that idol constantly, because there was a superstition that it fell out of heaven and therefore was worthy of honor. Let me tell you something about the Bible—it *did* come from heaven, but that statue *did not*. So believe the Bible and honor it.

3. Love It

If the Bible is all true, then we had better love it. The psalmist cried out, "Oh, how I love Your law!" (Ps. 119:97). And I love what it says in Psalm 19:10 as it speaks of the statutes of the Lord: "More to be desired are they than gold, yea, than much fine gold; sweeter also than honey and the honeycomb." In fact, verses 7–10 of Psalm 19 compose one of the most beautiful portions of Scripture. So if the Bible said it, believe it, honor it, and love it.

4. Obey It

We commented on this earlier, but if the Bible is true,

then we should obey it. Follow the admonition of 1 John 2:5a: "But whoever keeps His word, truly the love of God is perfected in him." If it's really what it claims, we should believe it, honor it, love it, and obey it at any price. It's interesting to see what Romans 6:16a says: "Do you not know that to whom you present yourselves slaves to obey, you are that one's slaves whom you obey?" If you yield yourselves as servants to God, you obey Him.

5. *Fight for It*

If the Bible is really true—fight for it! Jude 3 says, "Contend earnestly for the faith." "The faith" means "the body of revealed truth." The Greek for "contend earnestly" is *epagonizomai*, from which we get "agonize." Agonize for it; engage yourself in a battle to defend the Word of God. If it's really true, if it can do the things we said it could do, believe it, honor it, love it, obey it, and fight for it.

6. *Preach It*

In 2 Timothy 4:2a Paul simply said, "Preach the word." If it's really true—preach it. So if we are going to believe it, honor it, love it, obey it, fight for it, and preach it, then we must:

7. *Study It*

Paul says to Timothy in 2 Timothy 2:15, "Be diligent

to present yourself approved to God, a worker who does not need to be ashamed, rightly dividing the word of truth." "Rightly dividing" means "cutting it straight." Study it so you can interpret it properly—cut the text straight.

Paul was using the language of the ancient tentmaker. That craftsman made a tent out of a lot of different animal skins. He had to take every one of those animal skins and cut each piece properly so he could put the whole thing together. If he didn't cut every piece right, then the whole thing wouldn't fit together. In other words, Paul was saying that you can't have theology without exegesis. You can't have the true theology of Christianity unless you have the verses rightly interpreted, cut straight—and that takes study.

Charles Spurgeon said every Christian should study the Bible until his blood is "bibline." Do you know what they said about Apollos? In the New Testament they commended him by saying that he was "mighty in the Scriptures" (Acts 18:24). My prayer for you is that you study the Word of God, proclaim it, fight for it, obey it, love it, honor it, and believe it.

Review

1. What are the two kinds of obedience? Explain the differences between each one.

2. Why was Peter not supposed to go fishing as he did in John 21:3? What lesson was God teaching him when he couldn't catch any fish?

3. When Jesus questioned Peter's love for Him, why didn't Peter use the same word that Jesus used when he told him that he did love Him (John 21:15–17)?

4. To what did Peter appeal to prove to Christ that he did love him? Explain.

5. On what basis did Jesus accept Peter's loving commitment to Him?

6. When does God pour out His blessing and joy on the believer?

7. What is action fruit without the proper attitude fruit called?

8. Why is sorrow an important emotion for a believer to experience?

9. What does the Word of God give Christians victory over? How does it give us victory?

10. Why did God consider Satan's temptation of Christ a test? Why did Satan consider it a temptation (Matt. 4:1)?

11. What did Satan tempt Jesus to do in Matthew 4:3? How did Jesus respond (Matt. 4:4)?

12. What did Satan tempt Jesus to do in Matthew 4:5–6? How did Jesus respond (Matt. 4:7)?

13. How was Jesus able to command a legion of demons to come out of a man in Luke 4:33–36?

14. How is the Word of God like a sword?

15. What is the only way that Christians will know victory in their lives?

16. Why don't some Christians grow spiritually?

17. What are two prerequisites to spiritual growth? Explain each one.

18. What is the pattern of growth that is outlined in 1 John 2:13–14?

19. What do believers understand when they are at the first level of spiritual growth?

20. What is characteristic of the believer at the second level of spiritual growth?

21. What does Satan spend most of his time doing (2 Cor. 4:4)?

22. What is characteristic of the believer at the third level of spiritual growth?

23. What are some verses that show how the Bible is a resource for power?

24. What are some of the riches God has promised believers (Eph. 1:3–3:12)? What will happen when we learn those truths?

25. How is the Bible able to guide believers into God's will?

26. Since the Bible is the source of truth, happiness, victory, growth, power, and guidance, how should Christians respond? Explain each command.

27. According to 2 Timothy 2:15, why do we need to study the Bible?

Reflect

1. When God looks into your heart, what does He see? Does He see you obeying Him, but not wanting to obey? Or does He see that you have a sincere willingness to obey Him even when you fail? Are you experiencing happiness in your spiritual walk? If not, you may be obeying God without a true desire. Take this time to examine your heart. Honestly determine why you obey God. Ask Him to reveal your true desires. If there is any aspect of your spiritual walk that is not sincere, confess it to God right now. Ask Him to help you acquire the

desire to be obedient to Him in that area of your life.

2. Read Matthew 4:1–11 again. To pass the test that Satan gave Him, on three occasions Jesus quoted a specific portion of Scripture that dealt with Satan's attack. Would you be ready to defend yourself using God's Word if Satan were to attack you? Read 2 Timothy 2:15. You are to be able to handle the Bible accurately. What do you need to do to know it better? Commit yourself to that.

3. Reread the section on the patterns of growth from "child" to "young man" to "father." What level of growth are you presently at? How do you know? Why aren't you at the next level? What do you have to know better to ascend to the next level— God's Word or God Himself? What kind of commitment do you have to make to know His Word better? What kind of commitment do you need to make to know God better? Be faithful to maintain those commitments.

4. Review the seven responses to God's Word at the end of this chapter. Do you believe God's Word?

How is that manifested in your life? Do you honor God's Word? How do you manifest that? Do you love God's Word? How do you manifest that? Do you obey God's Word at any price? To improve your motivation for obedience, memorize 1 John 2:5. Do you fight for God's Word? How is that manifested in your life? Do you preach, teach, or communicate God's Word to others? Give some examples of people you have been able to minister to through God's Word. Only as you consistently study God's Word will you find that you will believe, honor, love, obey, fight for, and preach it.

3

WHO CAN STUDY the BIBLE?

In the nineteenth century there was a Danish religious philosopher by the name of Søren Kierkegaard. He said many things regarding Christianity and religion that we would not necessarily accept, but every once in a while he would say something rather profound. Let me quote one statement he made: "Too often in their church life people adopt an attitude of the theater, imagining the preacher is an actor and they his critics, praising and blaming the performances. Actually, the people are the actors on the stage of life. The preacher is merely the prompter, reminding the people of their lost lines."

I think he perceived a real problem. It's very easy for

people to come to church and treat it like a theater, and just sit and watch it happen. Then, they either praise or criticize what took place. But the purpose of a ministry in the pulpit is to stimulate the people in the pew. The reason I study and teach is to stimulate you to study and teach. But the sad part is that there are so many Christians who don't really get into it; they don't study the Bible, so they aren't able to teach it to somebody else.

A lady said to me at one of my conferences, "Do you know what your preaching does to me?"

I said, "I have no idea."

She responded, "It makes me want to study the Bible." She said it in a very matter-of-fact manner.

Then I said, "Well, I think that's the best compliment I've ever had, that it makes you want to study the Bible."

I really feel that's the whole point. My teaching is not to entertain. I do not preach to put on a show to be evaluated. I teach to stimulate you to do something on your own. And that is to learn the Word of God and live it. If you don't get that message, you miss the whole point.

And the sad part of it is there are so many Christians who don't really do that—they just don't get into it or teach it to somebody else. And there are always many distractions to studying and learning the Word.

No doubt there are difficulties and distractions in our busy culture, but that's not a good excuse. I think about Paul when he wrote to Timothy and said, "And the things that you have heard from me among many witnesses, commit these to faithful men who will be able to teach others also" (2 Tim. 2:2). In other words, "Timothy, what I told you, I want you to tell somebody else."

Paul had to encourage Timothy at this juncture in his life, because Timothy was having many difficulties, and he was beginning to falter. He was having anxiety, and Paul had written him about taking some wine for his stomach's sake (1 Tim. 5:23). People hassled him about his youth, so Paul had said, "Let no one despise your youth" (1 Tim. 4:12a), and, "Flee also youthful lusts" (2 Tim. 2:22). Timothy was fighting his youth, he was fighting his physical problem, plus, he was by nature a timid person. So Paul said, "For God has not given us a spirit of timidity" (2 Tim. 1:7a, NASB).

Some high-powered religious false teachers who had invaded the Ephesian church attacked Timothy. They were propagating genealogies and a philosophy that he apparently couldn't immediately refute. So Timothy was beginning to falter, but Paul said to him, "You can't stop now, too much is invested in you. Hold to everything that I committed to you, and give it to somebody else." That's the whole point. We can have victory over difficulties, and we need to share God's instruction with others.

Near the time I first preached a sermon in my church,

I had my father share a message with our congregation. He had made a great commitment in my life and had given me many things to pass on. His father had given him things to pass on. And what I have, I have to pass on. You have to take it, develop it, learn it and pass it on to somebody else. This is a relay race, and we're all involved.

Now let's consider some basic facts we need to understand as we address the question of "Who Can Study the Bible?" First, we must:

Know the Word

If we're going to study the Bible, we've got to be convinced that it *needs* to be studied. That seems to be basic, so let's look at some passages in Scripture that will help us understand it.

First there is Hosea 4:1–6. Hosea was facing the reality in Israel that God's people had abandoned Him. Consequently, they fell into all kinds of sin. They became an adulterous nation, violating their vow to God. But what was their basic problem? How did it happen? Why did it happen? Note what he writes beginning in verse 1: "Hear the word of the Lord, you children of Israel." Hosea puts his finger on the problem. When a nation ceases to hear the Word of the Lord, confusion and chaos take place.

He continues, "For the Lord brings a charge against the inhabitants of the land: 'There is no truth or mercy or knowledge of God in the land.' They had removed the foundation, and when the foundation was gone, what was left? Verse 2 gives us the answer: "By swearing and lying, killing and stealing and committing adultery, they break all restraint, with bloodshed upon bloodshed." In other words, you get national chaos when you give up the foundation of the Word of God.

In America today people are concerned about the condition of their country; they're concerned about a rising crime problem, the disintegration of the family, chaos in government and the economic stress and turmoil that results—people have all these concerns in their hearts. But there will be no resolution to any of these problems unless there is a reaffirmation of the Word of God as the absolute standard for this country.

Israel had failed in Hosea's day. When you destroy a biblical base, all you get is chaos. Everything bad had begun to happen because Israel would not hear the Word of the Lord. Verse 3 says, "Therefore the land will mourn; and every one who dwells there will waste away with the beasts of the field and the birds of the air; even the fish of the sea will be taken away."

Everything went wrong. Verse 6 sums it up for us: "My people are destroyed." But why? "For lack of knowledge; because you have rejected knowledge." When a society rejects the law of God and the knowledge of Him, people open the floodgates to chaos.

Proverbs 1:20–33 echoes this theme of the importance of knowing God's Word. As it is true in a nation, as in the case of Israel, it is also true in the life of an individual. If you do not have the Word of God as the base of your life, as the orientation for your behavior, as the solid foundation upon which you live—then there is no real base. The writer says, "Wisdom calls aloud outside; she raises her voice in the open squares." Then in verse 22: "How long, you simple ones, will you love simplicity? For scorners delight in their scorning, and fools hate knowledge." It says they turned a deaf ear and refused to hear (v. 24). Wisdom is available (vv. 23, 25, 33) and we must give attention to it, or reap the consequences.

Studying the Word of God is so important that it's the foundation of everything. A judge once wrote me and asked, "What does the Bible say about what is right in a court of law?" A doctor once asked, "What does the Bible say about what is right in terms of how we discipline our children?" Other doctors have written and asked, "What does the Bible say about abortion? What does the Bible say about euthanasia? What does the Bible say about how people are to be treated in certain psychological and psychiatric situations?" The Word of God is the standard! We can't live our lives rightly unless we have the knowledge of God's Word within us. So it's imperative that we be students of His Word.

Romans 12:2 reveals, "And do not be conformed to this world, but be transformed." But how do we as Christians rise above the corrupt system that engulfs us? How do we ascend beyond today's worldly mentality? Paul says, "Be transformed by the renewing of your mind, that you may prove what is that good and acceptable and perfect will of God." First, you must know the Word before you can live it. If you rush off trying to live life without the knowledge of God's truth, you're going to find yourself right in the middle of the world's system. This verse reiterates Ephesians 4:23, which also teaches us to "Be renewed in the spirit of your mind."

Several other passages of Scripture instruct us in this area, including:

"I pray, that your love may abound still more and more in real knowledge and all discernment" (Phil. 1:9, NASB).

"If there is any virtue and if there is anything praiseworthy—meditate on these things" (Phil. 4:8b).

"Increasing in the knowledge of God" (Col. 1:10b).

"But grow in the grace and knowledge of our Lord and Savior Jesus Christ" (2 Peter 3:18a).

"That the man of God may be complete, thoroughly

equipped for every good work" (2 Tim. 3:17).

"My son, eat honey because it is good, and the honey-comb which is sweet to your taste; so shall the knowledge of wisdom be to your soul" (Prov. 24:13–14a). In fact, all through the thirty-one chapters of Proverbs is the injunction to learn God's truth, to know it, to live it—and over and over again it tells us to seek wisdom. Every Hebrew boy, as he grew up, was taught the book of Proverbs so he might know God's standard for life.

Live the Word

As we come to know the Word, we must also live the Word. The knowledge of which Scripture speaks is not separated from obedience. Scripture knows nothing of theories. It knows nothing of the intellectualism of the Greek "wisdom" (*sophia*, or theoretical knowledge). The Hebrew idea of wisdom was always in the context of behavior. In fact, to the Jews, if you didn't live knowledge in accord with God's law, you didn't really know it. *Wisdom wasn't just a thought; wisdom was practical walking.*

So where the Bible draws us to knowledge, wisdom, understanding, enlightenment, and perception—it is always with a view toward behavior. You never really know something until you live it.

Several passages of Scripture expand our understanding of this vital principle:

"Blessed are those who hear the word of God and keep it!" (Luke 11:28).

"If you love Me, keep My commandments" (John 14:15).

"For this is the love of God, that we keep his commandments" (1 John 5:3a).

"Oh, that they had such a heart in them, that they would fear Me and always keep all My commandments, that it might be well with them and with their children forever!" (Deut. 5:29).

The Lord told Joshua that he was required to study and reflect on the Word of God. He said, "This Book of the Law shall not depart from your mouth, but you shall meditate in it day and night, that may observe to do according to all that is written in it. For then you will make your way prosperous, and then you will have good success" (Josh. 1:8). In other words, "Joshua, you must be committed to the law of God."

Chaos existed in Israel when the law was lost. Finally, when it was found, the people stood up and read it. A revival broke out because they had again found the standard for life (2 Chron. 34:14–32).

"For as the heavens are higher than the earth, so are My ways higher than your ways, and My thoughts than your thoughts. For as the rain comes down, and the snow from heaven, and do not return there, but water the earth, and make it bring forth and bud, that it may give seed to the sower, and bread to the eater, so shall My word be that goes forth from My mouth; it shall not return to Me void, but it shall accomplish what I please, and it shall prosper in the thing for which I sent it" (Isa. 55:9–11). God said, "As the rain and snow comes down and waters the earth, so My Word will come down and give growth to your life."

"I will worship toward Your holy temple, and praise Your name for Your lovingkindness and Your truth; for You have magnified Your word above all Your name" (Ps. 138:2). David was a man with a worshiping heart, and he worshiped God with these words: "God, I will worship You on the basis of Your truth." *We can't truly worship God, no matter how meaningful that might be in our own mind, unless we worship Him according to truth.* In John 4:24 Jesus says, "Those who worship Him must worship Him in spirit and truth." You can't devise your own means for worship. Like Saul, you can't offer the Lord a whole lot of animals that you stole against His commandment and then say, "Well, I'm serving the Lord" (cf. 1 Sam. 13:10–14). God doesn't want self-styled worship; He wants it according to His Word. *True worship is lived out in the lives of believers who love His Word.*

"Blessed are the undefiled in the way, who walk in the law of the Lord! Blessed are those who keep His testimonies, who seek Him with the whole heart! . . . Your word I have hidden in my heart, that I might not sin against You" (Ps. 119:1–2, 11). Psalm 119 is one of the most majestic poems in all of Scripture. Nearly every one of the 176 verses teaches us the necessity of obeying the Word of God.

So we find that the Scripture calls us to obey the Word. Passage after passage tells us of the importance of it as God's Word.

Can I ask you to make a covenant in your heart? I don't want to impose it on you. I just want you to do it because it's right. You may say, "Well, this Bible study is hard work." Yes, but these things were written "that your joy may be full" (John 15:11b). Do you want full joy in your life? That's why God wrote the Bible. This covenant I refer to was made by Josiah the king, and God really blessed him for it.

In 2 Chronicles 34:31 it says, "Then the king stood in his place and made a covenant before the Lord." This young man Josiah was like a beam of light in the midst of the darkness of ancient Israel. He was a godly man and he made a covenant before the Lord: "to follow the Lord, and to keep His commandments and His testimonies and His statutes with all his heart and with all his soul, *to perform the words of the covenant which were written in this book"* (emphasis added). Josiah said, "Lord, as long as I live, this day I vow to learn and to live Your Word." That's why he was different from everybody before him and after him. We can rise above the crowd too if we make that same covenant with the Lord. Are you willing to make that covenant?

Now to our main question: Who can actually study the Bible? I've said that everybody *should* study it, but who *can* study it and get something out of it? You might say, "Well, I'll have to go to a class or to seminary," or, "I'll have to get a lot of books to understand it." Will you really?

There are certain people who claim to understand the Bible, and they knock on your door and offer to explain it to you. But who can really understand the Bible? What are the basic requirements? In the remainder of this chapter, I'll share with you six requirements for who is able to understand the Bible.

REQUIREMENT ONE:
You Must Be a Believer

Bible study is hard work, but the first work that must take place is within your own heart. Apart from Christ, you will never comprehend His message.

Believers Can Understand

To understand the Bible, a person must be a true Christian. "You mean if you're not regenerate you can't understand the Bible?" That's right! In 1 Corinthians 2:10 we find a tremendous insight. It says, "But God has revealed them to us through His Spirit." The word "them" refers to God's truths, principles, or Word. But *who* receives them? Notice the little phrase "to us." That might not seem too important in the English, but it is important in the Greek because "to us" comes at the beginning of the sentence, which is the emphatic position. Paul is saying that the revelation of God's truth is "to us," and the "us" refers to believers. This is in contrast to the ones he has previously been referring to. From 1 Corinthians 1:18, to 2:9, he is talking about how ignorant the philosophers of the world are in regard to the truth of God.

But *why* can't they know the truth of God? Because it says in 2:9, "Eye has not seen." Worldly philosophers can't see it empirically—they can't find it out by discovery. Then, "nor have entered into the heart of man." They can't find it by their own feeling, or by their own emotion, or by their own musings, or by their own spiritual experience. God's truth is not available externally or internally, no matter how intelligent the philosopher might be.

Why? Because God has revealed it "to us," not to them. Paul says in verse 6 that there are those in the world who speak human wisdom—"the rulers of this age"—but none of these princes know the truth (v. 8). It's not available to them. Why? Because in their humanness they *can't* know it. Verse 11 says, "For what man knows the things of a man except the spirit of man which is in him? Even so no one knows the things of God except the Spirit of God."

If a person does not have the indwelling Spirit, he can't know the truth of God. He may think he knows some things, and he may try to figure some things out, but he can't truly know—at least not in the sense of knowing and living out that truth in life. But concerning Christians, verse 12 says, "Now we have received, not the spirit of the world." The "spirit of the world" is a synonym for human reason. Christians don't depend on human reason; we depend on "the Spirit who is from God." And because of Him we "know the things that are freely given to us of God."

Unbelievers Cannot Understand

The essence of the unbeliever is summed up in 1 Corinthians 2:14: "But the natural man does not receive the things of the Spirit of God, for they are foolishness to him; nor can he know them, because they are spiritually discerned." If you're not a believer, you cannot really perceive with understanding the truth of God. It is analogous to verse 11: A man cannot know anything about himself unless he knows it in his spirit. A dead body doesn't know anything because it has no spirit. Likewise, a person without the Spirit of God is like a physically dead body because he can't know anything spiritually. One prime aspect of spiritual death is the absence of the knowledge of God, because of the absence of the Spirit of God.

So, without knowing Christ you cannot know the Bible. That's what's so sad about alternative religious systems; they concoct elaborate theology, but they don't even know God to begin with and they deny Jesus Christ. Therefore, confusion is just added upon confusion, and the truth becomes hopelessly muddled. The truth is available only to those who know and love the Lord Jesus Christ.

Martin Luther once said, "Man is like a pillar of salt, he's like Lot's wife, he's like a log or a stone, he's like a lifeless statue which uses neither eyes nor mouth, neither sense nor heart until that man is converted and regenerated by the Holy Spirit. And until that happens, man will never know God's truth." So the essential on knowing the Bible is that you know God through Jesus Christ; the believing heart thus will understand God's Word.

Our Lord makes a profound comment in John 8:44 when He says to the Pharisees, "You are of your father the devil. . . . for he is a liar and the father of it." Then He says in verse 45, "But because I tell the truth, you do not believe Me." Amazing! The reason they didn't believe Him was because He told them the truth, and that was something they couldn't perceive. That is the state of unregenerate people. If you tell them the truth, they don't receive it because they *can't* perceive it.

However, I believe there is a point at which an unbeliever will become open to God. When he has a searching heart he says, "Lord, teach me Your truth. I want to know if Christ is real." If there's an open heart, there's a transition time when the truth is brought to the person and he or she is regenerated. In general, the natural man will never know the truth when he reasons from his own mind. Only when he opens his heart to be instructed by God and begins to seek Christ will the truth become evident. Then once he's converted, the Spirit will be within him to teach him the truth.

REQUIREMENT TWO:
You Must Be Diligent

In order to study the Bible we must be diligent. We can't study Scripture in a haphazard way—there has to be a commitment to it. Let's take a look at three key passages to see what I mean.

Acts 17:10–12

In Acts 17 the apostle Paul was moving around in his ministry to the Gentiles. He had been in Thessalonica, and he proceeded from there south to Berea. Beginning in verse 10: "Then the brethren immediately sent Paul and Silas away by night to Berea. When they arrived, they went into the synagogue of the Jews. These were more fair-minded than those in Thessalonica, in that they received the word with all readiness." Here were some open minds ready to receive the Word, "and searched the Scriptures daily to find out whether these things were so. Therefore, many of them believed." They were more noble than the rest because they were diligent in their study of the Scriptures.

I believe they were true saints who knew God under the terms of the Old Testament. Their hearts were cracked wide open when the gospel came in because they were open to receive it and they searched diligently. By the way, the word for "search" is a judicial term meaning "an investigation." They really got into it to see if Scripture was true. You can't study the Bible in a haphazard manner.

2 Timothy 2:15

In this verse Paul uses a tremendously strong word: "*Be diligent* to present yourself approved to God as a workman who does not need to be ashamed, accurately handling the word of truth" (NASB, emphasis added). You need to be hardworking and conscientious in your Bible study.

Why? So you can accurately handle it. If you don't, you'll have something to be ashamed of, and you will not be approved. The word "approved" is a great word. In the Greek it is *dokimos*, which means "proven, tested, shown to be of high quality." A high-quality Christian, an approved Christian, one who has no flaws for which he or she will be ashamed—this is a believer who is diligent to study the Word of God.

The words "accurately handling" ("rightly dividing" in the NKJV) mean literally "to cut it straight." Paul used these words because he made tents out of goatskins, and he had to cut the hides properly so they would fit together. He said you have "to cut straight" every portion of Scripture or the whole won't come together. You can't make sense out of the whole unless you know what to do with the parts. You must cut every portion of the Word of God straight and then fit the whole together. That takes work. As G. Campbell Morgan once said, "Ninety-five percent of inspiration is perspiration."

1 Timothy 5:17

"Let the elders who rule well be counted worthy of double honor, especially those who labor [work hard] in the word and doctrine." Paul uses *kopiaō* ("labor") here, which is a Greek verb that means "to work to the point of sweat and exhaustion." There has to be a commitment to diligence and hard work when you search the Scriptures.

If you're going to be a Bible student, if you're going to make a personal commitment to learn the Scriptures: First, you must know Jesus Christ as your Lord and Savior so you have the Holy Spirit to teach you. Second, you must be diligent.

REQUIREMENT THREE:
You Must Have a Great Desire

Third, and maybe this should be the apex of our thoughts, the ones who will understand the Bible are those who have a great desire to do so. Becoming a good Bible student will not happen by accident. You must desire it. Let's look at how the Scriptures illustrate this necessity:

Hunger for the Word (1 Peter 2:2)

"As newborn babes, desire the pure milk of the word, that you may grow thereby." A baby desires one thing—

milk. It doesn't care about anything else. It doesn't care
what the color of the curtains or the carpet is; it doesn't
care what the color of the nightgown it's wearing may be;
it doesn't care what car you buy—a baby wants milk. In-
fants have singlemindedness, and Peter said, "Like a baby
desires milk, and only milk, so should our hunger be for
the Word."

People sometimes ask me why our church studies the
Bible. A pastor will say, "Your church has grown from
Bible teaching. I'd like to do that and build a church." But
what they really want to do is use Bible teaching as a way
to build a church rather than as a fulfillment of their own
hunger. And it doesn't work as a gimmick. You must have
a *hunger* for the Word!

Seek the Word (Job 28:1–18)

I love what it says in Proverbs 2:4 regarding knowledge and understanding: "Seek her as silver." Can you
imagine how hard people work to find silver? That's the
way we ought to seek the knowledge of God's Word. In
Job 28 Job gives a tremendous discourse on mining, and
then he applies it to the Word. Beginning in verse 1:
"Surely there is a mine for silver, and a place where gold
is refined. Iron is taken from the earth, and copper is
smelted from ore."

He says men go to all lengths in mining. "Man puts

an end to darkness, and searches every recess for ore in the darkness and the shadow of death" (v. 3). He says they burrow into the earth like a bunch of moles, into pitch-black darkness, and they get themselves surrounded by very dangerous situations. They'll do anything to find what they're looking for. "He breaks open a shaft away from people; in places forgotten by feet they hang far away from men; they swing to and fro" (v. 4). The idea here is that of changing the configuration of the earth by mining and digging it all out. Verse 9 says they literally overturn the mountains by the roots. In verse 7 they go where no bird has ever been, and in verse 8: "The proud lions have not trodden it, nor has the fierce lion passed over it." They cut rivers among the rocks, and they dam up other places in verses 10–11. They do all of this digging to find a precious metal.

   In contemporary society, we dig and hunt and go to tremendous extremes to buy gold and silver to hang on our fingers, arms, necks, and ears. Just think of the tremendous expense involved. We mine for precious metals, and we go to great lengths to do so; yet, with all the advancement, and all the technology, and all the luxury, gold, and silver, the one thing we don't have is wisdom. Job points this out very clearly in verse 12: "But where can wisdom be found? And where is the place of understanding?" Where can we mine understanding?

"The deep says, 'It is not in me'; and the sea says, 'It is not with me.' It cannot be purchased for gold, nor can silver be weighed for its price. It cannot be valued in the gold of Ophir, in precious onyx or sapphire. Neither gold nor crystal can equal it, nor can it be exchanged for jewelry of fine gold. No mention shall be made of coral or quartz, for the price of wisdom is above rubies" (vv. 14–18). In other words, Job says that in humanity's earth, and in human economy, wisdom is not found. The implication is that mankind is foolish to spend such energy to find metal and then spend none to find truth. God help us to seek the wisdom in His Word as much as people seek precious metal from the earth.

Treasure the Word (Job 23:12b)

Do you have a desire for His Word? Do you have an overwhelming passion for His Word? Here's a great verse: "I have treasured the words of His mouth more than my necessary food" (NASB). If it came down to working for my food or studying the Bible, it would be His Word. If it came down to eating food or feeding on the Word, it would be His Word; for I treasure that above everything else. That's the kind of hunger the psalmist must have been referring to when he said: "O how I love Your law!" (Ps. 119:97, NASB). He says in Psalm 19:10b that the truth was "sweeter also than honey and the honeycomb."

So, we must have a great desire for God's Word.

But what if you don't have that desire? How then do you get it? Even if you don't seem to have the desire, all these requirements will come together. If you're born again, that's only the first requirement. If you're born again and diligent, those are just the first two. If you're born again, diligent, and you have a great desire, that's just three—but there are more. And if you're weak in one, it will be strengthened by another desire. What is the fourth requirement for who can study the Bible?

REQUIREMENT FOUR:
Those Who Are Holy

In order to study the Word of God, there must be holiness. Where do you get that? Let's look at two verses from Peter and James to help us define holiness.

1 Peter 2:1

"Therefore, laying aside all malice [Gk., *kakia*, 'general evil'], all deceit, hypocrisy, envy, and all evil speaking." In other words, clean up your act, maintain holiness, pursue righteousness, get your life pure, and then "desire the pure milk of the word, that you may grow thereby" (v. 2). If the desire isn't there, then you had better back up to verse 1. Do you see why I said you have to take them all together? If you're born again, and if you're holy and righteous (dealing with sin in your life by confessing it), out of that born-again reality and the holiness of your life will grow the diligent desire to study.

James 1:21

It says at the end of the verse, "Receive with meekness the implanted word." Receive with humility the Word. That's a great thought, but you can't do that unless you go to the first part of the verse: "Therefore lay aside all filthiness and overflow of wickedness, and receive with meekness the implanted word." The Word cannot do its work in a sinful life because it is not a conceptual thing; it is a living reality. It isn't just thought; it's life.

So what is the Word of God saying to us? Who can study the Bible? Someone who is born again; someone who is willing to be diligent and search the Scripture; someone who has a strong and hungering desire for it— a desire that is born out of holiness and righteousness.

REQUIREMENT FIVE:
You Must Be Spirit-Controlled

In order to study the Word of God effectively, you must be Spirit-controlled. How wonderful it is to study the Scripture and know that I not only have the page in my hand, but I have the Author in my heart. The Author and Teacher is the Spirit of God. First John 2:20 says, "But you have an anointing from the Holy One, and you know all things." Just stated by itself that verse may not make a lot of sense, but let me give you the context. John was talking about false teachers—antichrists. The Gnostics, who were a group of people who thought they knew everything (Gk., *gnōsis*, "to know"), said, "We know because we have an anointing." They thought they had a special anointing that elevated them above everybody else. But John said to the Christians, "You're the ones with the anointing. You don't have some mystical Gnostic anointing; you have an anointing from the Holy One, and you know all things."

In verse 27 he expands further on the same thought: "But the anointing which you have received from Him abides in you." What is this anointing that lives in us? It's the Spirit of God. And since the Spirit of God lives within us, we don't need human teachers because *He* teaches us. John said that we don't need teachers to teach us human wisdom. Why? Because we have an anointing—the Spirit of God.

It's obvious then that we need to be born again, be diligent, have a strong desire, live a holy life, and be Spirit-filled—Spirit-controlled because the Spirit is the One who teaches and applies the Word to our lives. But there's one final requirement for those who can study the Bible.

REQUIREMENT SIX:
You Must Be Prayerful

All of these other requirements must come together in an atmosphere of prayer. You could even draw a circle around the other five requirements and encompass them with prayer. I believe our Bible study must be born out of prayer. When I study the Bible I pray this simple prayer: "Lord, as I approach your Word, show me Your truth and teach me what I must know." I would never approach the Scripture without first seeking God in prayer.

Paul, in Ephesians 1:15–18a, says, "I . . . do not cease to give thanks for you, making mention of you in my prayers: that the God of our Lord Jesus Christ, the Father of glory, may give to you the spirit of wisdom and revelation in the knowledge of Him, the eyes of your understanding being enlightened; that you may know." Paul says, "I'm praying for you." What are you praying for, Paul? "That you'll know, that your eyes will be open, that you'll understand, and that you'll see the truth." If Paul prayed for us to understand God's Word, then we are well instructed to pray as he did.

Who can study the Bible? You must be the right *who* or the *how* won't matter. Are you born again? Do you have a strong desire in your heart? Are you diligent? Holy? Spirit-controlled? Prayerful? If you are, then you can open the pages of the Bible, and God will reveal His truths to your heart. When your life is right, then the method of how to study the Bible will become productive and life-changing as you implement it.

Review

1. What is the purpose of the preacher's ministry from the pulpit?

2. What were some of the problems that Timothy faced in his ministry? What did Paul encourage him to do (2 Tim. 2:2)?

3. What happens when a nation ceases to hear God's Word (Hos. 4:1–2)?

4. What kind of foundation does a person have if he doesn't have God's Word as his base?

5. How can a Christian rise above the corruption of the world system (Rom. 12:2)?

6. What injunction is scattered throughout the thirty-one chapters of Proverbs?

7. Describe the differences between the Greek and Hebrew concepts of wisdom. Which concept does the Bible follow?

8. What is the only way we can truly worship God (John 4:24)? How is that manifested?

9. What is the main thing Psalm 119 teaches?

10. What was the covenant Josiah made in 2 Chronicles 34:31?

11. Who are the only people who can understand the Bible? Why can't anyone else understand it (1 Cor. 2:9–14)?

12. How is a person without the Spirit of God like a dead body?

13. What was the response of the Pharisees when Jesus told them the truth (John 8:45)?

14. What is the only way that the natural person can ever begin to know God's truth?

15. Why were the people in Berea more noble and fair-minded than those in Thessalonica (Acts 17:10–11)?

16. The Bereans searched the Scriptures (Acts 17:11). What does that mean?

17. Why do we need to be diligent in our study of the Bible? Explain (2 Tim. 2:15)?

18. How hard should you work at your Bible study (1 Tim. 5:17)?

19. What should Christians be like in their hunger for God's Word (1 Peter 2:2)?

20. What does Proverbs 2:4 say about how we should seek knowledge and understanding?

21. To study the Bible a person must be holy, but

how does he or she become holy? How will that
help their desire to study God's Word (1 Peter
2:1–2)?

22. Who teaches us when we study the Bible (1 John
2:20, 27)?

23. What is the first thing a believer should do before he or she starts to study God's Word (Eph.
1:15–18)?

Reflect

1. The Hebrews associated wisdom with behavior,
whereas the Greeks conceived of it as an intellec-
tual exercise. When you learn some spiritual truth,
are you like a Hebrew or a Greek? Do you put that
truth into action, or do you merely meditate on it
as good instruction without applying it? What
spiritual truths are you very familiar with that you
have yet to put into practice? Be honest in your
analysis. Make a list of those truths. Next to each
one, indicate how you plan to put it into practice in
the next week. Once you have started, be committed to faithfully practicing them until they become
part of you.

2. In 2 Chronicles 34:31 Josiah made a covenant "to walk after the Lord, and to keep His commandments and His testimonies and His statutes with all his heart and with all his soul, to perform the words of the covenant written in this book" (NASB). Are you willing to make that same covenant with God? Begin that covenant by first memorizing 2 Chronicles 34:31.

3. Many Christians honestly have trouble with their desire to study God's Word, but here is a way to increase that desire: pursue holiness. Look up the following verses and write down what they teach about holiness:

- 2 Corinthians 7:1
- Ephesians 4:21–24
- 2 Timothy 2:21–22
- 1 Peter 1:14–16
- 2 Peter 1:5–8.

According to 2 Peter 1:5, what do you need to add to virtue (or moral excellence)? What is the only way to obtain that? But what must you first add virtue to? Be faithful to be holy in all your behavior, and your desire to study God's Word will increase.

4. The most important thing to do before you study the Bible is to pray. It also should be the last thing you do. Right now, thank God for the things He has taught you through this particular study. Ask Him to help you apply the truths He has taught you. The next time you get ready to study the Bible, be sure to ask God to teach you those truths that will be most applicable to your spiritual walk. Thank Him right now for the treasure that His Word is in your life.

4

HOW TO
STUDY
the BIBLE

I don't know if you've ever really thought about the magnificence of the Bible and what a privilege we have in studying it, but I hope because of this study you'll be able to focus in on some of the tremendous things that await you in the Scripture as you open it up.

Some time ago I read an illustration that went like this: The Bible is like a magnificent palace constructed of precious Oriental stone, constituting sixty-six stately chambers. Each one of these rooms is different from its fellows and is perfect in its individual beauty; yet, when viewed as a whole, they form an edifice—incomparable, majestic, glorious, and sublime.

In the book of Genesis, we enter the vestibule, which immediately introduces us to the records of the mighty works of God in creation. This vestibule gives access to the law courts, the passage way to the picture gallery of the historical books. Here we find hung on the walls scenes of battles, heroic deeds, and portraits of valiant men of God. Beyond the picture gallery we find the philosopher's chamber (the book of Job), passing through which we enter the music room (the book of Psalms). Here we linger, thrilled by the grandest harmonies that ever fell on human ears. And then we come to the business office (the book of Proverbs), in the very center of which stands the motto: "Righteousness exalts a nation, but sin is a reproach to any people" (14:34).

Leaving the business office, we pass into the research department—Ecclesiastes. From there we proceed into the conservatory (the Song of Solomon), where the fragrant aroma of choicest fruits and flowers and the sweetest singing of birds greet us. Then, we reach the observatory where the prophets with their powerful telescopes are looking for the appearing of the Bright and Morning Star prior to the dawning of the Son of righteousness. Crossing the courtyard, we come to the audience chamber of the King (the gospels), where we find four lifelike portraits of the King Himself that reveal the perfections of His infinite beauty. Next, we enter the workroom of the Holy Spirit (the book of Acts) and, beyond, the correspondence room (the epistles), where we see Paul, Peter, James, John, and Jude busy at their tables under the personal direction of the Spirit of Truth. And finally, we enter the throne room (the book of Revelation), which enraptures us by the mighty volume of adoration and praise addressed to the enthroned King, which fills the vast chamber; while the adjacent galleries and judgment hall portray the solemn scenes of doom and wondrous scenes of glory associated with the coming manifestation of the King of kings and Lord of lords.

O the majesty of this Book, from creation to the culmination! How it behooves us to be diligent in our study.

But *how* do we go about it? How can we really understand the Bible? In this chapter, I'll give you four foundations for authentically understanding God's Word for your daily life.

FOUNDATION ONE: Read the Bible

Bible study begins with reading it. But quite frankly, a lot of people never get to that point. They sort of nibble at it, but they never really read it. They may read a lot of books *about* it, but they don't really read the Bible. *There is no substitute for reading the Scripture.* We must be totally committed to reading it because that's where it all begins. My suggestion is that you try to read through the Bible once a year.

First, let's discuss how we should read.

The Old Testament

I believe Christians should try to read through the Old Testament once a year. There are thirty-nine books in the Old Testament, and if you read about twenty minutes a day, you should be able to get through it in one year.

The Old Testament was originally written in the Hebrew language (and some Aramaic), which is a very simple language. It doesn't have the lofty concepts of Greek thinking; it isn't a theoretical language; it isn't a conceptual language; and it isn't a philosophical language with a lot of abstraction. It's a very simple, very concrete language. In fact, as a student in seminary, I found the study of Hebrew infinitely easier than the study of Greek. It is just not a complex language.

You can read through the narrative of the Old Testament, for the most part, year after year, and all the while build a comprehension as you read. I would also suggest that as you read the Bible, mark in the margin a notation where you don't understand what it's talking about. If you do that, you'll find an interesting thing will happen. As time goes on you will begin to check them off your margin, because as you read and reread the Old Testament from Genesis to Malachi, an understanding will become yours that will answer some of those questions you had. The ones you don't answer in your reading, you can use for individual study with a commentary or other source to find the meaning. But begin by just reading it. Don't become overwhelmed and think, "How can I ever learn the meaning of every verse?" Just begin to read through the Old Testament at least once a year.

I remember in seminary Dr. Charles Feinberg, who was a great mentor of mine and a wonderful man of God who knew so much about the Old Testament, used to baffle the students. One of them would sometimes try to trap him and say, "Dr. Feinberg, what's in 1 Kings chapter 7 verse 34?" He'd sort of mumble it in his mind in Hebrew, translate it, and tell us what was there.

He said to me one day, "I try to read a book a *day* just to keep up on things."

I said, "What kind of a book?"

"Any book, a book on art, a book on history, a book on somebody's life, any book. One a day so that I can stay up with things."

I said to him, "With all of your reading a book a day and all of your study of the Hebrew language and writing commentaries and teaching a full load of classes, do you have time to read the Bible?"

He answered, "I read the Bible. I read through the Bible four times a year, and I have for I don't know how many years."

That's where it all begins. There's no substitute for reading the Bible.

The New Testament

I have a little different plan for reading the New Testament. And by the way, I think our major thrust should be reading the New Testament. I believe that's scriptural. In Colossians 1:25–26 Paul says, "Of which I became a minister according to the stewardship from God which was given to me for you, to fulfill the word of God, the mystery which has been hidden from ages and from generations, but now has been made manifest to His saints." Paul said, "I'm called by God to give you the mystery that has been hidden."

Now the mystery, basically, is the New Testament revelation. Paul also said that he was an apostle of the "mystery" in Ephesians 3:3–5. So the major thrust of his ministry was the new revelation. He would allude to the Old Testament insofar as it illustrated and elucidated and supported the New Testament.

The message of the New Testament is the culmination of revelation. It is that which embodies and engulfs all that was in the Old Testament. In a sense, the New

Testament will summarize for you the content of the Old Testament, as well as lead you further into the fullness of revelation. So when you read the New Testament you must spend more time in it because it explains the Old Testament. Also, it is written in the Greek language, which is a more complex, perhaps more difficult language to understand than the Hebrew because it talks more in abstractions and concepts, rather than narrative stories. For this reason we need a greater diligence in studying the New Testament. Here's how I've done it.

My method when I was in seminary was to read 1 John every day for thirty days. You can do it this way, too. The first day just read 1 John all the way through. It will take you only twenty-five or thirty minutes. The idea is to read it through the first day, then on the second day read it through again; on the third day, read it through again; on the fourth day, read it through again; on the fifth day, read it through again. Just sit down and read it. Now about the seventh or eighth day you're going to say to yourself, "This is getting old. Besides, I've got this stuff pretty well under my belt." But that's the tough part. If you push through and just stick with it for thirty days, you'll have a tremendous comprehension of 1 John.

Basically, this is what I do all the time. As I prepare messages, I just read through the particular Bible book over and over again until the whole book fills my mind in a kind of visual perception. I would also suggest that you take a three-by-five card and write down the major theme of each chapter. Then, every day when you read the book, just look at the card and read through the list. You'll soon begin to learn what's in the chapters.

When you've finished reading 1 John for thirty days, where do you go next? I suggest you go to a large book in the New Testament (and remember, all the time you're still reading the narrative of the Old Testament twenty minutes a day). I believe you should go from 1 John to the gospel of John. "But that's twenty-one chapters!" That's right, so just divide it into three sections. Read the first seven for thirty days, the second seven for thirty days, and the third seven for thirty days. At the end of those ninety days you will have pretty well mastered the content of the gospel of John. And you've also had a three-by-five card on the first seven chapters, one on the second seven, and one of the third seven. So you've memorized the major theme of each chapter. But what does this method of Bible study really accomplish?

There is great merit to it. I remember when I started using this approach I was really amazed at how fast I began to retain the things in the New Testament. I had always wanted to make sure that I didn't wind up a "concordance cripple," never being able to find anything in the Bible and having to look up the verses in the back. And to this day, the gospel of John, 1 John, and the other books of the New Testament have stuck in my mind. Why? Because this is how we learn. Isaiah said you learn line upon line, precept on precept, here a little, and there a little (Isa. 28:10, 13). When you study for a test, you don't pick up your book, read through the notes once, and say, "I've got it!" (At least not if you're normal.) You learn by repetition, repetition, repetition. That's the same way to learn the Bible.

After the gospel of John you might want to go to Philippians, another short book. Then you might want to go to Matthew, and then to Colossians, then to Acts. Divide it up like that, back and forth, a small book and a large book. "But that's going to take a long time!" No. In approximately two and a half years you will have finished the whole New Testament. You're going to read the Bible anyway, so you might as well read it so you can remember it. Some people may say, "Well, I have my devotions, and I read a passage for the day." That's fine. But if I asked you, "What was it?" you may say, "Well, let me think. . . ." What if I asked, "What did you read three days ago?" Having the answer may be next to hopeless. It's really difficult to retain anything by moving fast. You must go over it and over it and over it. If you believe the Bible is the living Word, it will come alive in your life as you read it in a repetitious manner.

Many people have asked me if I think they should always read from the same Bible translation. My answer to that is generally, yes. Stay with the same version so you will have familiarity. Once in a while it's good to read the passage from another version just to further explore it. I normally read in the *New American Standard Bible* (for many years I read from the King James Version), but just for my own edification I'll invariably use the *New King James Version* or the *English Standard Version* to read the passage I'm studying. I think those two are the best available comparative translations.

Reading the Bible answers this question: What does the Bible say? We have to read it to find out exactly what it says. Let me tell you another interesting thing that happens when you begin to read the Bible repetitiously. You will find that your total comprehension will increase incredibly. That's because the Bible explains the Bible.

"A resource that will help you see how one part of the Bible explains another part of the Bible is *The MacArthur Study Bible* (Word, 1997). This book goes through the entire Bible and gives you explanatory notes and cross-references that help explain the meaning of a particular text." So, when you begin to read the Bible, your new understanding will fill in a lot of the gaps. After all, God did not write a book to confuse you. The Bible is not a book that's supposed to have some kind of hidden truth—it's not a secret book. You're supposed to discover what God is trying to say.

But some people will say, "Whatever you do, don't read the book of Revelation; it's so confusing." But it says, "Blessed is he who reads and those who hear the words of this prophecy" (1:3a). It's not that difficult. But I'll tell you one thing, you'll never fully understand Revelation unless you're reading through Daniel and Isaiah and Ezekiel. It all begins to come together when you read the whole Word of God. You will be amazed at what will take place in your life.

The first foundation for *how* to study the Bible, then, is to *read it*.

FOUNDATION TWO:
Interpret the Bible

There are some people who don't interpret the Bible; they just apply it. They read it and go directly to applying it without interpreting it. They simply don't bother to find out what it really means. Our first foundation was to *read* the Bible. That will answer the question: What does the Bible say? The second foundation, *interpret* the Bible, answers the question: What does the Bible mean by what it says? We have to interpret the Bible. We can't take the Bible like an aspirin. It is not a tablet. We can't just say,

"Well, I had my devotions, and I was reading along, and I just decided this is what it means." No. You have to *know* what it means.

In Nehemiah 8 we have an interesting passage: "Now all the people gathered together as one man in the open square that was in front of the Water Gate; and they told Ezra the scribe to bring the Book of the Law of Moses, which the LORD had commanded Israel. So Ezra the priest brought the Law before the assembly of men and women and all who could hear with understanding on the first day of the seventh month. Then he read from it in the open square that was in front of the Water Gate from the morning until midday" (vv. 1–3a). Now this is where it all begins—you have to read the Bible.

Continuing in verse 3c: "And the ears of all the people were attentive to the Book of the Law." Then in verses 5–6: "And Ezra opened the book in the sight of all the people, for he was standing above all the people; and when he opened it, all the people stood up. And Ezra blessed the Lord, the great God. Then all the people answered, 'Amen, Amen!' while lifting up their hands. And they bowed their heads and worshiped the Lord with their faces to the ground."

The people responded to the reading of the Word by worshiping the Lord. But verse 8 is the key: "So they read distinctly from the book, in the Law of God; and they gave the sense, and helped them to understand the read-ing." Do you see what that says? That's why we must not only read the Word, we must also seek to know what it means by what it says.

In 1978 I had the opportunity to attend the Inter-national Council on Biblical Inerrancy. Approximately 250 great scholars from around America came together in Chicago. They wanted to reaffirm to the entire world that every word of God is pure, as Proverbs 30 says. They wanted to affirm to the whole world that the Bible is the absolute truth of God, inerrant in its very words. For four days they gave papers, papers so erudite that I couldn't even understand all of them. It was tremendous scholar-ship, and we were carrying around these huge notebooks with terrific theological papers in them.

At the end of the conference I taught a seminar ti-tled, "How Does Inerrancy Relate to the Ministry of the Church?" I said this: "It is amazing to me that in a con-ference on inerrancy where everybody is stressing how important every word is in the Bible, that nobody has given an expository message which deals with every word. In other words, why are we fighting for every word if we never bother to teach every word or to learn what they mean?"

It's not enough to just say, "We believe every word is true," and then pick only one word out of forty-five verses and preach a sermon on that one word. That's why the only ultimate end of a true commitment to the inerrancy of Scripture is exposition of its entirety, as it was given by God.

So we have to come to, "What does the Bible mean by what it says?"

I really think that in many ways answering that question has been the key to the growth of Grace Community Church. People were in the dark for so long and we just kind of cracked the door of understanding open for them. It isn't that tough to open the Bible's door because God has given us His Word to understand and His Spirit to be our teacher.

In 1 Timothy 4:13 Paul told Timothy how to preach. He said, "Till I come, give attention to reading, to exhortation, to doctrine." Do you see what he meant? He told Timothy to read the text, explain the text (doctrine), and apply the text (exhortation). You just don't read it and apply it; you read it, then explain it, and then apply it. That's what "rightly dividing the word" (2 Tim. 2:15) is all about. Otherwise, misinterpretation is the likely result, and misinterpretation is the root of all kinds of problems.

For example, let me mention some things that people teach today based on misinterpretation. First, some people are teaching that since the patriarchs practiced polygamy, so can we. Or, since the Old Testament sanctioned the divine right to the king of Israel, all kings have divine rights. Or, since the Old Testament sanctioned the death of witches, we should be killing witches. Or, because some Old Testament plagues were from God, we should avoid sanitation so we don't thwart Him. How about this one? The Old Testament teaches that women would suffer in childbirth as a divine punishment, therefore, no anesthetic should ever be used. These are all misinterpretations because somebody doesn't understand what the Bible is really saying, and they don't understand the situation in which it was written.

I understand that it isn't necessarily easy to understand all of the Bible. I remember a Bible teacher who once told me, "I'm so sick of trying to understand the Bible that I've decided to take everything for everybody. I've tried the dispensational route, I've tried the modified dispensational route, and I've tried the covenant theology route. So I've just decided to apply everything to everybody."

I said, "Oh, when did you sacrifice your last lamb? Do you go through ceremonial washings of all the pots in your kitchen before your wife prepares your kosher meal?" You can't apply everything to everybody. There must be proper interpretation.

But how do I get the proper interpretation? Let me show you some areas you need to understand.

Errors of Interpretation

To accurately interpret the Word, there are three errors to be avoided. First, *don't make a point at the price of
proper interpretation.* In other words, don't make the Bible
say what you want it to say.

That's like the preacher who preached that women
shouldn't have hair on top of their heads. His text was
"Top Knot Come Down" from Matthew 24:17 where it
says, "Let him who is on the housetop not come down."
Such a ridiculous lesson is *not* what that passage is
teaching.

Or, you can approach the Bible like the guy who said,
"I've already got a sermon; I just have to find a verse for
it." That's having a preconceived idea and then getting
some verses to support it. I know if I try to *make* a sermon, I wind up forcing the Bible to fit *my* sermon. But if
I try to comprehend a passage, out of the understanding
of that passage flows a message. You can think of some
great stuff and some fabulous outlines, but then you have
to twist the Bible to make it say what you want it to say.

Let's look at a couple of examples. I remember reading in the Talmud that one time the rabbis decided they
wanted to preach a message that the people should care
for each other. They had a social problem because people
weren't loving other people. So they said the best illus-

tration in the Bible to show that people should love one another is the story of the Tower of Babel. The Talmud interprets it this way: the reason God scattered all those people, and the reason He confounded their language, was because they had put material things before people. As the Tower of Babel was growing taller, the rabbis noted, it took a sod carrier many hours to carry the load of bricks to the top so the bricklayers could lay their bricks. If a man fell off the tower on the way down, nobody paid any attention because they didn't lose any bricks. But if a man fell over on the way up, the bricklayers were furious because they lost their bricks. So that's why God scattered the nations and confounded their language, because they were more concerned about bricks than people. Well, it's true you should be more concerned about people than bricks, but that's not what the Tower of Babel teaches us. God did not scatter them because they were more concerned about bricks. He scattered them because they were building an idolatrous religious system.

I've also heard sermons from 2 Peter 2:20 on how you can lose your salvation. Invariably, they'll quote the verse: "For if, after they have escaped the pollutions of the world through the knowledge of the Lord and Savior Jesus Christ, they are again entangled in them and overcome, the latter end is worse with them than the beginning."

Then they'll say, "You see, you can escape the pollutions, you can have the knowledge of the Lord and Savior, and you can fall and become entangled, and your latter condition is worse than before you believed. You see, you can lose your salvation."

However, the thing they forget about is the word "they." If you study the word "they" from the beginning of 2 Peter 2, you'll find that it's talking about "wells without water," "clouds carried by a tempest" (v. 17), and "spots and blemishes" (v. 13). If you trace it back to 2:1 you'll see that it's talking about false prophets who follow the doctrines of demons. You cannot use the verse to prove that a person can lose his or her salvation, because that is not its context.

In fact, Paul has a word for those who do this. In 2 Corinthians 2:17a he says, "For we are not, as so many, peddling the word of God." The Greek word for "peddling" is *kapēlos*, which basically had to do with selling something in the marketplace deceitfully; selling a product that really wasn't what it was claimed to be, or falsifying. Paul said there are some who falsify the Word of God; they adulterate it to fit their own thoughts.

You must not make the Bible illustrate your sermon or your thoughts. Be careful not to interpret the Bible at the price of its true meaning—let it say what it means to say.

Second, *you must avoid superficial interpretation.* As

you study the Bible to learn what it says; don't be superficial. Some people will say, "Well, I think this verse
means . . ." or, "What does this verse mean to you?" Un-
fortunately, a lot of Bible studies are nothing but a col-
lection of ignorance; a lot of people sitting around telling
what they *don't* know about the verse. I'm all for Bible
studies, but somebody has to study to find out what a
passage really means; *then* you can discuss the application. First Timothy 5:17 even tells us about elders who
work hard at the Word of God. So it's important not to
be superficial.

A third caution regarding Bible interpretation is *you
must not spiritualize*. The first sermon I ever preached was
a horrible sermon. My text was "And the angel rolled the
stone away." My sermon was "Rolling Away Stones in
Your Life." I talked about the stone of doubt, the stone of
fear, and the stone of anger. That is not what that verse
is talking about; it's talking about a real stone. I made it
a terrific allegory. Once I heard a sermon on "they cast
four anchors . . . and wished for the day" (Acts 27:29 KJV);
the anchor of hope, the anchor of faith, and so on. Those
were not anchors of anything but metal. I call that "Little Bo Peep" preaching because you don't need the
Bible—you can use anything to give a text meaning. You
can even use the nursery rhyme character Little Bo Peep.

Let me show you what I mean. Someone can get up

and say, "Little Bo Peep has lost her sheep." All over the world people are lost (you see, you don't need the Bible). "And can't tell where to find them. And they'll come home—" Ah, they'll come home all right. Then you tell a tear-jerking story about some sinners who came home "wagging their tails behind them." Spiritualizing is so easy to do, and a lot of people do it with the Old Testament. They turn it into a fairy-tale book and make all kinds of crazy interpretations. Don't spiritualize the Bible; get the right meaning.

Sources of Interpretation

To properly interpret the Bible, we'll have to bridge some gaps. To do that, we'll have to examine the sources of interpretation.

The Bible has been around for many years, parts of it for as long as four thousand years. How are we going to understand what the authors were saying and the various circumstances in which they lived? We have to bridge four gaps.

First, we have to understand *the language gap*. (We speak English, but the Bible was written in Hebrew and Greek, plus a few parts in Aramaic, which is similar to Hebrew.) Otherwise, we won't fully be able to understand the Scripture. For example, in 1 Corinthians 4:1 the apostle Paul says, "Let a man so account of us, as of the ministers of Christ" (KJV). When we think of the English word *minister*, we think of a prime minister or the minister of defense. A minister is an elevated position; it's a dignified term. But the Greek word is *hupēretēs*, which means a third-level galley slave on a ship. Paul said that, when the record goes in for him, let it be said that he was nothing more than a third-level galley slave for Jesus Christ. You would never get that out of the English term. Why? Because there's a language gap.

Another example is in the book of Hebrews. When you look at the word *perfection* in the book (e.g., 6:1; 7:11), you can get completely confused on how you comprehend Hebrews unless you understand that there perfection has to do with salvation, not spiritual maturity. That's what you'll find out as you study the words and their relationships in the text. It is very important to do this. And to study the words in the Bible, particularly in the New Testament, I highly recommend *Vine's Complete Expository Dictionary of Old and New Testament Words* (Thomas Nelson, 1996; an older public domain version for the New Testament version is available online for free at www.tgm.org/bible.). It's very helpful for someone who doesn't know Greek. You can look up every English word, and it will tell you the Greek meaning. It will be a great help to you as a Bible student. Also, a good concordance will help you in the study of words.

The second gap is *the cultural gap*. The cultural gap must be bridged because cultures can be very different. If we don't understand the culture of the time in which the Bible was written, we'll never understand its meaning. For example: "In the beginning was the Word, and the Word was with God, and the Word was God" (John 1:1). What does that mean? Why didn't he say, "In the beginning was Jesus"? Well, he used "the Word" because that was the vernacular at that time. To the Greeks the term *Word* was used to refer to a kind of ethereal, spatial energy that was floating around. John said to the Greeks that this floating cause, the thing that caused everything, that spatial energy, that cosmic power, is none other than the Word that became flesh (1:14).

To the Jew, the term *Word* was always the manifestation of God, because "the Word of the Lord" was always God emanating His personality. So when John said "the Word was made flesh and dwelt among us," he was identifying Jesus Christ, the incarnate Christ, as the very emanation of God. In the text, therefore, he meets both the Greek *and* Hebrew mind with the right word that each can identify with at vital points.

This continues all through the Bible. If you don't understand the Gnosticism existent at the time of the writing of Colossians, you won't understand the book. If you don't understand the culture at the time the Judaizers were moving into the Gentile churches, you can't understand the book of Galatians. If you don't understand the Jewish culture, you can't understand the gospel of Matthew. There must be cultural comprehension to fully understand the Bible.

Some helpful books in this area are *The Life and Times of Jesus the Messiah* by Alfred Edersheim (Eerdmans, 1974) and *The New Manners and Customs of Bible Times* by Ralph Gower (Moody, 2005).

There are also *geography gaps* that we must bridge. When we read in the Bible that people went *down* to Jericho, what does that mean? Well, when you go into Jericho you go *down*. When it says they went *up* to Jerusalem, it is because Jerusalem is definitely *up*, on a high plateau. In 1 Thessalonians 1:8 it says, "For from you the word of the Lord has sounded forth, not only in Macedonia and Achaia, but also in every place. Your faith toward God has gone out." What's amazing is that the Thessalonians' faith sounded out so fast. Paul had just been there, and when he wrote the letter, very little time had passed. Paul had been with them for a couple of weeks, but their testimony had already spread far. How could that happen so fast? If you study the geography of the area, you'll find that the Ignatian Highway runs right through the middle of Thessalonica. The city was the main concourse between the East and West, and whatever happened there passed all the way down the Ignatian Highway's line of communication. Do you see how a little bit of geographic understanding enriches your comprehension?

Finally, there is *the gap of history*. When you know the history behind a passage, that history will also help your comprehension. In the gospel of John, the whole key to understanding the interplay between Pilate and Jesus derives from a knowledge of history. When Pilate came into the land with his emperor worship, it infuriated the Jews and their priests. So he was off to a bad start from the very beginning. Then he tried to pull something on the Jews, and when they caught him, they reported him to Rome, and he almost lost his job. Pilate was afraid of the Jews, and that's why he let Christ be crucified. Why was he afraid? Because he already had a rotten track record, and his job was on the line.

That's the kind of history we need to understand to open up the meaning of the Bible. And you can get this kind of information from various sources. One is *The Zondervan Pictorial Encyclopedia of the Bible* (Zondervan, 1976). Or, a good Bible dictionary will help.

To interpret the Bible means closing the gaps. As you interpret the meaning of Scripture by using various sources, you will close the three gaps mentioned above. But what are the principles you should use?

Principles of Interpretation

Besides the *sources* of interpretation, you must also understand the *principles* of interpretation in order to understand the Bible accurately. To do so involves five specific principles.

First, you should use *the literal principle*. That means you should understand Scripture in its literal, normal, natural sense. There will be figures of speech, but that's normal language. There will be symbols, but that's normal language too. When you study apocalyptic passages, such as in Zechariah, Daniel, Ezekiel, Isaiah, and Revelation, you will read about beasts and images. Those are figures of speech and symbols, but they convey *literal* truth. Interpret the Bible in its normal, natural sense. Otherwise, you're taking an unnatural, abnormal, nonsensical interpretation. For example, the rabbis said that if you take the consonants of Abraham's name, b-r-h-m, and add them up, you get 318. Therefore, when you see the word Abraham, it means that he had 318 servants. That's *not* what it means. It simply means Abraham.

So we must take the literal, normal, natural interpretation. We have to be careful when somebody comes along and says there's a secret meaning—and they use the verse "For the letter kills, but the Spirit gives life" (2 Cor. 3:6b). They use an allegorical method to get the hidden, secretive meaning. Do you know what that is?

Nobody knows! They make it up. Don't do that—interpret Scripture in its literal sense.

The Bible must also be studied according to *the historical principle*. What did it mean to the people to whom it was spoken or written? It is said that a text without a context (historically) is a pretext. You have to understand the historical setting in many cases, or you'll never really understand what's in the writer's heart.

This includes many of the gaps mentioned earlier, as well as biographical information regarding the human author of the biblical book and the date of the book's writing. Many resources are available to help in this area. Many of these are included in *The MacArthur Study Bible*. More details on the background of historical context regarding New Testament books can also be researched through the MacArthur New Testament Commentary Series (Moody Publishers).

Third, we must understand *the grammatical principle*. To study the grammar we must look at the sentence and parts of speech, including the prepositions, pronouns, verbs, and nouns. In school we had to learn how to diagram a sentence so we could find out what it was saying. For example, in Matthew 28:19–20 we have the Great Commission: "Go therefore and make disciples of all the nations, baptizing them . . . teaching them to observe all things that I have commanded you." As you first read it, "Go" sounds like a verb; "make disciples, baptizing, teaching," all sound like verbs. But as you study the sentence, you find there's only one verb, *mathēteusate*, "make disciples." "Go," "baptizing," and "teaching" are nothing more than participles, which means they modify the main verb. What the Great Commission says is "make disciples," and in making disciples you will have to go, baptize, and teach. When you understand that, the fullness of Jesus' command comes out of the text.

Another illustration appears in Matthew 18:20. How many times have you heard somebody say this in a prayer meeting: "'Where two or three are gathered together in my name, I am there in the midst of them.' Friends, two or three of us are here, so the Lord is here"? But if I'm there *alone*, the Lord is still there. That verse has nothing to do with a prayer meeting. If you study the context and the grammar you find that out. It's actually saying that when you discipline somebody, when you put somebody out of the church, and his sin has been confirmed by two or three witnesses, then Christ is in your midst. So you have to examine the grammar carefully to fully comprehend the meaning of the text.

Fourth, there is *the synthesis principle*. This is what the Reformers called the *analogia scriptura*—the Scripture all comes together. In other words, one part of the Bible doesn't teach something that another part contradicts.

So, as you study the Scripture, it must all fit together. For example, when you're reading through 1 Corinthians and you come to 15:29, in which Paul talks about the baptism for the dead, do you say, "Well, there's a new idea. You can get baptized for a dead person and that will save him"? But does the Bible actually allow for somebody to be baptized for a dead person? Where is that in Scripture? Doesn't that contradict the doctrine of salvation? That can't be the interpretation of that passage because no passage, in and of itself, will contradict the teaching of Scripture. That's the synthesis principle.

J. I. Packer has wonderfully said, "The Bible appears like a symphony orchestra, with the Holy Ghost as its Toscanini, each instrument has been brought willingly, spontaneously, creatively, to play his notes just as the great conductor desired, though none of them could ever hear the music as a whole. . . . The point of each part only becomes fully clear when seen in relation to all the rest" (from *God Has Spoken*).

That tells me there are *no* contradictions in the Bible. What appear as contradictions can be resolved if we have the information, because the Bible comes together as a whole.

But maybe you are thinking, "This is all so foggy, the literal principle and all these other things. When does it ever get down to where I'm living?" The final question is:

So what? As you try to interpret the Bible, how do you find out what it means for your life? Make sure that in your Bible study you find *the practical principle*.

I have a little phrase that I use: "Learn to principlize the Scripture." Read it and find out what spiritual principle is there that applies to you. But you can't do that until you've gone through the other principles first: literal, historical, grammatical, and synthesis. You know what it means by what it says—now you come to how it applies to you.

So that's how you interpret the Bible. While you're reading through the Bible, now and then work on some of the problem passages. Read a little in a Bible dictionary, or a commentary, and begin to put some things together. What is the literal meaning? What is the historical setting? What is the grammatical structure? How does it fit in with the rest of Scripture? and, How does it apply to me?

FOUNDATION THREE:
Meditate on the Bible

Don't be in a hurry when you study God's Word. Deuteronomy 6:6–7 says, "And these words which I command you today shall be in your heart. You shall teach them diligently to your children, and shall talk of them when you sit in your house, when you walk by the way, when you lie down, and when you rise up." In other words, you ought to have God's Word running around in your mind all the time.

If you're reading through the Old Testament, and if you're reading a book of the New Testament through thirty times in a row, all the time, then you're going to have it running around in your mind. Meditation is what takes all of those parts and begins to mold them together into a cohesive comprehension of biblical truth. God also says in Deuteronomy 6:8–9, "You shall bind them as a sign on your hand, and they shall be as frontlets between your eyes. You shall write them on the doorposts of your house and on your gates." God says He wants His Word everywhere—"I want it in your mouth, when you stand up, lie down, walk, and sit. I want it in front of your house, on your gates, I want it on your arms, hanging between your eyes—I want it everywhere!"

But we live in a culture in which we drive down the street and moral garbage constantly assaults our eyes— alcohol ads, pornography, crude humor—and the filth in turn pours into our heads. But God said we should take His Word and let *it* be the billboard in front of our eyes, let it be filling our mind and our voice wherever we go.

A man was asked one time, "When you can't sleep, do you count sheep?" He said, "No. I talk to the Shepherd." That's what God wants His people to do, talk to the Shepherd—meditate. Psalm 1:1–2 says, "Blessed is the man who walks not in the counsel of the ungodly, nor stands in the path of sinners, nor sits in the seat of the scornful. But his delight is in the law of the Lord; and in His law he meditates day and night." Like the cow chewing its cud, just going over it and over it and over it, so too should we meditate on the Word, going over it and over it and over it.

FOUNDTATION FOUR:
Teach the Bible

Finally, we are to teach the Bible. The best way to learn Scripture is to give it away. I've found that the things I learn well enough to teach are the things I retain. But do you know that it's very easy to *not* be understood? If you hear somebody speak and you don't understand anything he says, then *he* probably doesn't understand his subject. But it's hard to be clear, because to be clear you have to master your subject. As a teacher, you are forced to master your subject. Then if you teach, you'll retain it. Just feed somebody else and see how it feeds your own heart. I believe that personal motivation for study comes from responsibility. If I didn't have somebody to teach, I wouldn't produce.

My prayer is that these words help you get started in

studying God's Word more deeply. Read the Bible, interpret the Bible, meditate on the Bible, and teach the Bible. But when you think you've done it all, don't become proud and say, "I've arrived. I've mastered it all." Just remember Deuteronomy 29:29a: "The secret things belong to the Lord our God." When you've said it all, done it all, and learned it all, you haven't scratched the surface of the infinite mind of God. But do you know what the purpose is? Your purpose in learning the Word of God is not to have knowledge for the sake of knowledge, because Paul said, "Knowledge puffs up" (1 Cor. 8:1a). Your purpose is to *know* God, and to know God is *to learn humility.*

Review

1. What does Bible study begin with?

2. Describe a good method for reading through the Old Testament.

3. What is the "mystery" Paul referred to in Colossians 1:26? What was the major thrust of his ministry?

4. Why is it important to spend more time when reading the New Testament as compared to the Old Testament?

5. Describe a good method for reading a book in the New Testament.

6. What is a good way to learn anything, particularly the Bible?

7. Why is it good to continue reading from the same version of the Bible?

8. What will happen when you begin to read the Bible repetitiously?

9. What question does Bible interpretation answer?

10. What did the people of Israel do in Nehemiah 8:8?

11. What did Paul command Timothy to do in 1 Timothy 4:13? What did he mean?

12. How did the Talmud misinterpret the story of the Tower of Babel? What is the correct interpretation?

13. How do some people misinterpret 2 Peter 2:20? What is the correct interpretation?

14. What does Paul say about those who try to make the Bible fit their way of thinking (2 Cor. 2:17)?

15. Why is it important to avoid superficial interpretations?

16. Give an example of spiritualizing a passage of Scripture.

17. Give some examples that illustrate the language gap we face when we study the Bible.

18. What is one good way of bridging the language gap?

19. How does John 1:1 illustrate the cultural gap that exists between our day and the first century?

20. Give an illustration of how an understanding of the geography of the day is important to our interpretation of the Bible.

21. What gap needs to be closed to understand the interplay between Pilate and Jesus?

22. What is the first principle we should use in interpreting the Bible? Explain.

23. Why is it important to know the historical context of a passage of Scripture?

24. Explain the grammar of Matthew 28:19–20.

25. Explain the synthesis principle of Bible interpretation.

26. As you interpret the Bible, how do you find out what it means for your life?

27. According to Deuteronomy 6:8–9, where does God want His Word?

28. What is the best way to learn what the Bible says?

Reflect

1. Make up a plan for reading both the Old and New Testaments. Decide what time or times of the day you want to set aside for reading. Start in Genesis for your reading in the Old Testament. Pick any book in the New Testament for your daily reading. Just be sure to break it down if necessary so you can read for thirty minutes each day for thirty days. Begin your reading schedule today.

2. If you have been wanting to study a particular portion of Scripture but didn't know how, now you can. Plan the time that you want to spend on your study. If you don't have some of the study tools mentioned in this chapter, you may want to visit a library. In your study, be sure to avoid the errors of interpretation. As you study, work at bridging the linguistic, cultural, geographical, and historical gaps. Finally, use the proper principles of interpretation as you study. Remember, the goal of your study is not only to learn what the Bible means, but also to learn how it applies to you.

SCRIPTURE INDEX